THE HEART OF THE TEMPLE

A personal journey through God's house

THE HEART OF THE TEMPLE

ANNE LE TISSIER

Foreword by Jennifer Rees Larcombe

Published 2006 by CWR, Waverley Abbey House, Waverley Lane, Farnham, Surrey GU9 8EP, England.

See back of book for list of National Distributors.

Front cover image: Photodisc
Concept development, editing, design and production by CWR.
Printed in Finland by WS Bookwell

ISBN-13: 978-1-85345-379-3
ISBN-10: 1-85345-379-X

CONTENTS

PART THREE

The Temple in Heaven

FOREWORD

A few years ago, when I was organising a Prayer Retreat in the Welsh Hills, I asked Anne Le Tissier if she would lead one of the morning sessions.

When she told me she wanted to 'take us on a tour of Solomon's Temple', I have to admit I did wonder how she hoped to use a rather boring sounding academic study of an Old Testament building to help us find greater intimacy with God in our lives today!

My misgivings rapidly evaporated as the morning progressed. Anne's eyes shone with enthusiasm as she showed us that all the endless details about measurements and materials were not as dull and irrelevant as most of us had previously thought!

'When we realise that God cared so much about every tiny detail of what the temple looked like and how it was constructed, it shows us just how much He cares about every single aspect of our lives too – because nowadays He does not live in a building, He lives in *us*! Every area and object in the temple has something vital to teach us about prayer and the way God wants us to live our lives in Him. By the end of that morning we had all 'caught' her fascination and the temple seemed anything but dull!

'You really ought to write about all this,' I urged her.

Some years later, when the book was finally finished, we were celebrating together over a pot of tea when I asked her,

'How did this passion for the temple begin for you?'

'The seed was planted in my heart fourteen years ago,' she replied. 'I was walking through the streets of Sydney, Australia, a week before Christmas in the pouring rain. It was a period in my life when I was not looking after myself very well, and I was exhausted, cold, wet and very hungry. I had just gone into a café and bought a mug of tea when I distinctly heard God say, "Do you not know that your body is a temple of the Holy Spirit, who is in you, whom you have received from God? You are not your own; you were bought at a price. Therefore honour God with your body" (1 Cor. 6:19). I had not been a Christian very long and I had no idea that verse existed. Thinking of my body as God's temple was a totally new idea to me and it led me to find out everything I could about the temple in Jerusalem and the portable tabernacle, which preceded it.'

This book is the fruit of all those years of study; Anne not only uses the illustration of the temple to show us how God delights to live in us and wants to make us fit to be His residence by beautifying us in body, soul and spirit, but she does something more. Paul tells us that we should 'live, move and have our being in God' (Acts 17:28) but it is hard to know how this is possible in today's pressured world with all its distractions and interruptions. Anne is one of the busiest people I know yet she has discovered the secret, which she shares with us in small, daily bite-sized pieces. This book has to be one of the most fascinating I have ever read and it comes with my highest recommendation.

Jennifer Rees Larcombe
October 2005

PREFACE

> Solomon gave orders to build a temple for the Name of the LORD … Do you not know that your body is a temple of the Holy Spirit, who is in you, whom you have received from God? You are not your own; you were bought at a price. Therefore honour God with your body' (2 Chron. 2:1; 1 Cor. 6:19–20)

If you were given the choice of spending some time either watching paint dry or reading the chapters in 1 and 2 Chronicles detailing the dimensions and building of the Jerusalem Temple, I wonder which one you would choose. Over the years I've heard countless comments referring to the mundane nature of these passages describing the work that David and Solomon undertook for God's temple. In fact, I gather that a recent edition of the Bible has been published which actually omits them as they are perceived to be so uninspiring, and presumably irrelevant, for today's modern readership!

It is therefore my desire to share with you through the pages of this devotional handbook the relevance which the temple's preparations, construction, ministry and purpose continues to have for Christians living in the twenty-first century. This may come as a surprise for those of us who acknowledge Jesus' perfect sacrifice for sin which removed the need for a stone temple and sacred priesthood as a means for people to approach and worship God. Nevertheless, as this reflection reveals, the principles of temple ministry remain in Scripture because they continue to be an important guide for our knowledge of and service to God today. The material is relevant for anyone who is new to the faith as well as those who've known Jesus as Lord for many years. It develops our understanding of Old Testament history, but also provides principles, challenges and inspiration to encourage all of us to a life of purer consecration, devotion to God and ministry as He intended – no matter at what stage we are in our journey of faith. Furthermore, you can use it on your own as a personal devotion or within a group setting. I trust, therefore, that this instructive reflection will encourage you to see your own life as a temple to house God's Holy Spirit, which in turn may inspire any necessary changes of habits, priorities, motives and so on, to conform to that role.

Despite higher literacy rates, reading is on the decline owing to the busy, often stressful schedules put upon many of us in today's western culture. Such a lifestyle invariably leaves little or no time and energy for the luxury of reading a book, without being disturbed, made to feel guilty or nodding off to sleep! Consequently, it has been my aim to minimise the length of chapters and break them down into manageable, bite-sized chunks, enabling readers to take in as little or as much as they are able to at each sitting.

I make no apology for the copious references to Scripture – some of which are quoted in full but many of which are simply left as chapter and verse. It is not expected that you look up each and every one of them (unless you feel so inclined), but they're included as a means to support the material under review.

After this preface you will find a simple diagram outlining the gates, boundaries and courts of the Jerusalem Temple at the time of Jesus. Do remember to refer to this as you develop your own image of how God's wonderful dwelling-place might once have been. The book itself is then written in three parts.

- Part One provides a two-chapter backdrop to the history of the temple in Jerusalem, explaining why it was built in the first place and how it was transformed to a living bodily temple.
- Part Two comprises the main body of study applying historical facts to aspects of faith today. For example, the foundations apply to the basis of faith, the altar raises the subject of choice and living sacrifices, the building materials relate to diet, the sanctuary applies to prayer, the exquisite decor to physique and reputation, the priestly service to our work, ministry, responsibilities and so on.
- Part Three concludes the book with a short meditation on the temple in heaven and eternal life thereafter.

Each chapter includes sections called 'The Tale of the Temple' outlining the temple's history; 'Temple for Today' which applies that history to our own lives; and concluding pages in which to reflect on the theme under review. The term '*Selah*' is often written within verses of the Psalms – a Hebrew word that urges the reader to pause and take time to ponder what has been written. The *Selah* pages are just that – places to pause and reflect on what you have read and how you might engage with it in your own life before moving on to the next chapter. To help you there are also two journal pages after Chapters 2, 29 and 30 on which you might wish to write down your thoughts and prayers as a result of your meditations and how God may be speaking to you.

But before we return to Eden to find out where it all began, may I take this opportunity to express my sincere thanks to CWR who have encouraged me to write this book; to my selfless, inspiring husband who is a beautiful expression of God's love to me and who supports me wholeheartedly as I pursue God's dreams in my heart; to my dear mother who read the first draft and provided such a helpful, gentle critique; to my lovely daughter for her patience as I constantly disappeared out of sight to engross myself for hours with my laptop; to Jennifer Rees Larcombe, my precious mentor whose wonderful influence, nurturing and guidance has been an invaluable blessing; and to many other close friends and family members who I cannot name for the lack of space available, but who have all stood by me in bringing this project to birth – you know who you are and I thank you.

But above all, I acknowledge my dearest friend who made this possible in the first place, who has inspired me with it over the last fourteen years, who has taught me how to start putting it into practice in my own life and has sat with me hour after hour to help me encourage others do likewise through these pages: to Jesus, the Son of the Most High God, the perfect temple of God's Holy Spirit – I give all the thanks, all the honour and all the praise.

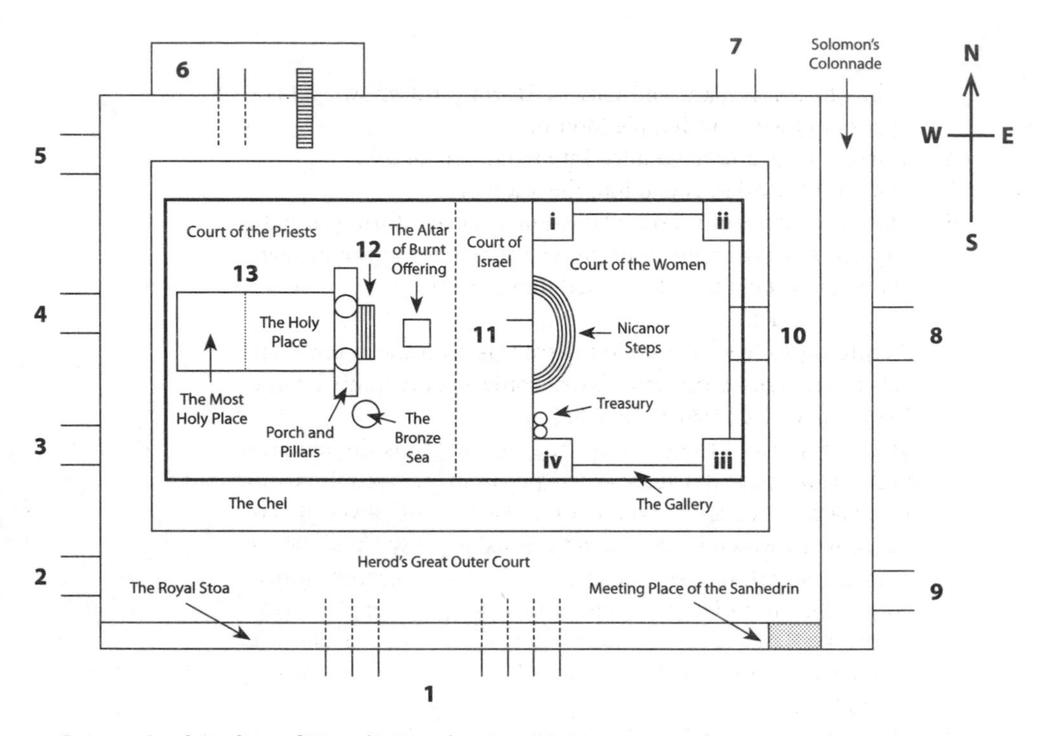

Summarised Outline of Herod's Temple, *circa* AD 30, not to scale

For Herod's Temple, an extended outer court was built, which surrounded the inner courtyards and sanctuary.

While there is some difference of opinion concerning the names and position of gates, the Temple Mount boundaries may have been as follows:

1. The Holdah Gates in the southern wall formed one double and one triple gate. Access was by way of low openings in the wall into tunnels that sloped upwards, coming to the surface well inside the interior of the court.
2. Barclay's Gate, which connected with Robinson's Arch, descended by stairs into the lower suburb, a place frequented by the poor inhabitants of the Tyropoeon Valley.
3. The principal western gate of Kiponos opened onto the magnificent Royal Bridge, now called Wilson's Arch. It was a massive construction of arches that spanned the Tyropoeon

Valley to connect the old City of David (also known as the upper city) with the Temple Mount.

4. Warren's Gate also descended into the lower suburb.
5. The West Gate descended into the lower city.
6. The Tower of Antonia housed the Roman Guard during Herod's day, accessing the outer court by way of a subterranean passage and a set of stairs that descended into the northern porches of the outer court.
7. According to Jewish tradition there was a northern entrance called the Tadi/Tedi/Terdi Gate. Some believe it to be the Benjamin or Upper Gate (Jer. 20:2).
8. The east wall was the same as the city wall. Thus the temples built by Solomon, Zerubabbel and Herod all included the same East Gate, which looked out upon the Mount of Olives. It was the route by which the red heifer was led on the annual day of atonement and was the gate in Ezekiel's vision through which God's glory both left and then returned to the temple (Ezek. 11:23; 43:4). Today it is called the Golden Gate; in Herod's Temple it was the Shushan Gate, in Solomon's the East or the King's Gate.
9. The Horse Gate was built in Herod's Temple where Solomon's stables would have been situated.
10. The Beautiful Gate leading up into the Court of the Women from a 15-foot wide terrace called the *chel*.
11. The Nicanor Gate leading into the Court of Israel.
12. Twelve steps leading up to the sanctuary.
13. The veil separating the Holy Place from the Most Holy Place.

There were various chambers in the Court of the Priests but just four in the Court of the Women:

i. Chamber for cleansed lepers to wash themselves.
ii. Chamber to store wood for the altar of burnt offering.
iii. Chamber for the Nazarites to make their preparations.
iv. Chamber to store oil and wine for the offerings.

PART ONE

IN THE BEGINNING

1 THE NEED FOR A TEMPLE

'They will know that I am the LORD their God, who brought them out of Egypt so that I might dwell among them.' (Exod. 29:46)

The Tale of the Temple

- God created a beautiful garden in Eden where He walked with Adam and Eve (Gen. 3:8).
- Tragically, however, their sin polluted the perfect paradise, banishing them from God's presence (Gen. 3:23).
- God determined to restore His habitation with humankind, first in a portable tabernacle – a beautifully constructed tent (Exod. 25:8–9); and then within a stone temple, built and completed by Solomon in 959 BC,[1] on Mount Moriah in Jerusalem (2 Chron. 3:1).
- The temple was destroyed after the Babylonians took Israel into exile but reconstruction work was later initiated under orders of King Cyrus of Persia, and supervised by Zerubbabel (Ezra 1:1–2:2).
- Following further destruction, King Herod the Great ordered the rebuilding of the last temple in 19 BC. Not that he was a God-fearing man, but its construction sought to appease subjected Israel while its magnificence impressed the Romans. It took 46 years to complete (John 2:20).

Temple for Today

'If anyone loves me, he will obey my teaching. My Father will love him, and we will come to him and make our home with him.'
John 14:23

Home is the habitat of the heart. It is the imprint of individuality, a picture of personality, a testimony of taste.

I wonder what mix of decor, furnishings, rooms, people, music and environment makes you feel at home. Is it pastel or bright, plain or striped, dark or light? Is it organised mess or everything put away in its rightful place? Do you just sweep floors when visitors arrive or do you pick up fluff from clean carpets? Do you write messages in the dust to your family or wipe it away every morning? Did you introduce 'the creased look' or do you even iron the underwear?

God makes His home in every believer's heart – a living, breathing, walking, talking temple of Yahweh. He too has certain preferences concerning His home, but to what extent do we adhere to them? Is He at ease or uncomfortable with His surroundings; pleased or perturbed with the landlord; Master or Guest in that which is rightfully His?

In Part Two, we'll contemplate how to apply the principles of God's stone temple to His living temple – principles of building, maintenance, service and worship. But, before we don the overalls, take up the paintbrush or start the cement mixer, let us consider why an omnipresent God required this holy temple in the first place. Perhaps that will then encourage us to apply its purpose today.

In the beginning

In the beginning – a time before Internet technology, travel and commerce; before architecture, cultures and language; before telephones, books and art; before men, women, animals and plants; a time before the world began – God was and God reigned. He who would breathe life into the first tick of time was moving, roaming, hovering over the deep, potent with purpose on the brink of command.

'And God said ...'

That which was not, was created, and 'Thus the heavens and the earth were completed in all their vast array' (Gen. 2:1).

Nevertheless, even within that perfect profusion of creation, nothing surpassed the boundless magnitude of immutable love the Creator yearned to share with the created. Placing Adam and Eve in a garden with shelter, nourishment and work, He talked and walked with them, taught and cared for them. Eden had no need for a temple, for God and His children lived in perfect harmony. Man and woman, made in His own image and likeness, were destined from the outset for divine intimacy but theirs was the choice to reciprocate.

Disaster!

Spinning on its flawless axis the perfect world was set for eternity until one act of disobedience sent it reeling off course. God's eyes are too pure to look on evil (Hab. 1:13), His holiness is all consuming. He could have abandoned, even destroyed humankind, but He loved them so much that He shed the blood of an animal in their place, using its skin to cover the shame of their sin (Gen. 3:21). It was the first lesson of sacrifice, the springboard of God's strategic plan to get rid of the evil instigator and restore harmony forever.

'"You must not eat from the tree of … knowledge"… she took some and ate it … and he ate it. Then the eyes of both of them were opened …'
Gen. 2:17; 3:6–7

To satisfy His yearning

I'm not sure I'd have ever come to faith if my God stood aloof until the end of time. Not that anyone can yet see Him face to face (Exod. 33:20) but owing to His tremendous love for us, His reconciliation plan included ways for Him to dwell with us during His process of restoration.

It all began with an old and wrinkly, childless nomad called Abram (later called Abraham), to whom God promised a nation of descendants and a land of their own, out of which He would birth His means of reconciliation for all people. But Abraham's descendants had to promise in return that they would obey God's covenant Law – godly commandments that taught them how to live holy lives.

'I will make you into a great nation and I will bless you … and all peoples on earth will be blessed through you … To your descendants I give this land …'
Gen. 12:2–3; 15:18

The Law could not eradicate the sinful nature but it did provide a means of disciplining it, thereby guiding God's people into upright and godly lives in contrast to their pagan neighbours. But they, like us, weren't perfect and as the consequence of sin is death (Rom. 6:23), they required some kind of atonement to approach their holy God; something that made amends for their wrongdoing.

'He is to lay his hand on the head of the burnt offering, and it will be accepted on his behalf to make atonement for him.'
Lev. 1:4

And so, by developing a system of animal sacrifice to make such amends, and consecrating a priesthood to seek mercy on their behalf, God's timeless yearning to be among His people could, at least in part, be satisfied. Descending in all His glory He filled Moses' wilderness tabernacle – a portable tent of fine linen, goats' hair and animal skins.

From tabernacle to temple: 1, 2 and 3

'Then have them make a sanctuary for me, and I will dwell among them.'
Exod. 25:8

Both tabernacle and later temple were significant symbols of God's presence among His people as they travelled through the wilderness then settled in the promised land. Scripture reveals the rise and fall of three temples built by Solomon, Zerubbabel, then Herod the Great. One temple followed another, simply because the priests and people digressed from following God's ways, so making themselves vulnerable to enemy attack (2 Chron. 7:19–20).

If you've visited Jerusalem, you may have seen the last remaining evidence of Herod's Temple – the western wall or *Wailing Wall*. It's a traditional site for Jewish pilgrims to lament its downfall and seek Yahweh in prayer, but its story doesn't stop there. Paul, the apostle, bridges the gap of understanding between the old and the new, reaffirming God's ongoing desire to live with His people. But rather than using a temple of stone, He lives in a temple of flesh, blood and bone (1 Cor. 6:19–20) – temporary dwellings until we see Him face to face.

But before moving on, take time for *Selah* – to pause and to ponder the marvel of God's ways. It's tempting to skimread the history of the temple, so losing its significance for our New Testament, 'westernised', Gentile Christianity; but as both Jesus and Paul referred to it in post-resurrection terms it must still have much to teach us, some 2,000 years since being destroyed.

The temple was an awesome set of buildings with exquisite decoration worthy of its Lord. It housed all manner of activities in its divine worship and ministry to the people, but its fundamental purpose was to be a temple for sacrifices and a house of prayer (2 Chron. 7:12; Isa. 56:7) – the means for God to dwell with His people and the mode for them to worship.

Selah

Come with me and rest awhile within the temple courts …

Run your hand along vast slabs of stone, down cool marble pillars, across fine linen ephods – handle the bronze utensils and razor-sharp knives.

Listen to the bleating lambs and fluttering feathers of doves cooped up in cages; the exchange of temple currency and rabbis teaching the Torah.

A trail of smoke from the vast altar twists gracefully over the sanctuary, dispersing an aroma of roasting meat.

Inhale the fragrant incense as reverent priests pass by – don't you just long for a slice of their serenity to cope with your own busy day?

… Now close your eyes to distraction and let God reveal His presence to you within this magnificent dwelling-place …

This temple – its reverent worship, prayer, sacrifice, ministry, teaching, splendour, priestly service, reputation and so on – is God's desire for your life. How does that make you feel?

Almighty, all-loving God, I am overwhelmed by Your eternal longing to live with me – thank You for making that possible through the temple and then through Christ. Please bring alive Your Word to my heart as I learn more about my stone and marble predecessor, Amen.

2 THEREFORE …

'Jesus answered them, "Destroy this temple, and I will raise it again in three days" … But the temple he had spoken of was his body.' (John 2:19,21)

The Tale of the Temple

- Jesus insinuated that He was the reason the significance of the temple in Jerusalem would diminish as the means of forgiveness and worship (Matt. 12:6).
- God confirmed His Son's claims. As Jesus died, the heavy curtain that prevented anyone but the high priest from entering the Most Holy Place tore in two from top to bottom. It symbolised the change to the new covenant by which any believer from any nation may approach God in prayer through faith in Jesus (Matt. 27:50–51).
- Indeed, Jesus is the sacrificial lamb of this new covenant and the High Priest in heaven, who, by His own blood, enters God's presence and daily intercedes on our behalf (Heb. 7:23–28; 9:11–15).
- Consequently, the old earthly tabernacle and temple became obsolete, but the infilling of believers with the Holy Spirit at Pentecost established a new one (Acts 2:3–4; 1 Cor. 3:16).
- Until perfection is restored in the new heaven and earth, Jesus is the cornerstone, not of a stone temple, but of all believers of every nation, being built together to become a dwelling-place in which God lives by His Spirit (Eph. 2:19–22).

Temple for Today

God loves you ...

If nothing else from the last chapter, remember this – God has loved you since creation to the cross to eternity. History confirms that nothing can dissuade His love for you (Rom. 8:38–39). To awaken each morning to that unfathomable truth has power to transform your life, purpose, motives, dreams, self-worth and so much more. For such is the extent of God's love that He wants constantly to live with you – to dwell by His Spirit within the depths of your being.

In light of this though, we may need to make some suitable adjustments to furnish our lives appropriately as the residence of God's Holy Spirit.

'The LORD appeared to us in the past, saying: "I have loved you with an everlasting love; I have drawn you with loving-kindness."'
Jer. 31:3

'Within your temple, O God, we meditate on your unfailing love.'
Psa. 48:9

... therefore honour God with your body

> In a large house there are articles not only of gold and silver, but also of wood and clay; some are for noble purposes and some for ignoble. If a man cleanses himself from the latter, he will be an instrument for noble purposes, made holy, useful to the Master and prepared to do any good work. (2 Tim. 2:20–21)

I too have a number of bowls at home. There is one in which I clean muddy walking boots and, dare I say, it's the one placed by the bed when I'm not feeling too well! I have another in which I wash dishes because dung-encrusted boots are a tad too unhygienic for dinner plates. Finally, there is an especially clean one in the bathroom in which I wash my body.

Being filled with the Holy Spirit redefines our life as a holy sanctuary but does not automatically consecrate our lifestyles. I would not dream of washing my face in the sick bowl any more than I'd clean dinner plates along with the walking boots; neither, therefore, should I expect God to feel at home in a temple tarnished by incongruous attitudes and inappropriate behaviour.

> Do you not know that your body is a temple of the Holy Spirit, who is in you, whom you have received from God? You are not your own; you were bought at a price. Therefore honour God with your body. (1 Cor. 6:19–20)

Herein lays the rationale of this book, Paul highlighting an obligation to honour God with our body – the vessel encompassing every aspect of our lives. It is a sacred sanctuary, 'therefore' we are obliged to use it with reverence for God.

Temporary phenomenon or lifetime pursuit?

Inviting God's Spirit into our lives is an awesome experience that may cause a flurry of 'spring-cleaning' in honour of His arrival. But while spring-cleaning is a helpful seasonal or house-buying activity, it's the daily washing-up and sweeping out dirt that keeps the house in order.

Furthermore, the arrival of God's Spirit is not a temporary phenomenon – He continues to live in the life of a believer no matter our inevitable behaviour slips. Nevertheless, His Word and historical evidence of the Jerusalem Temple's ministry provide a plethora of principles for godly living that we might radiate the glory of the One who lives within.

'What then? Shall we sin because we are not under law but under grace? By no means!'
Rom 6:15

All kinds of regulations monitored temple ministry but our freedom from that law is not a licence for liberalism. We are made holy in God's sight through Christ's redemptive blood (Heb. 10:10) and are holy temples by nature of His indwelling holiness – but God calls us to live holy lives to be in harmony with the ways of His Spirit (1 Pet. 1:15–16).

Many of us have certain habits and behaviour patterns that crop up regularly on the confession list; annoying idiosyncrasies that we just can't seem to break. But engaging with the practical and spiritual implications of being God's temple brings a unique dignity to life, one that unleashes God's motivation to throw out ungodly practices. And this is by no means 'mind over matter', but releasing the potential of Almighty God dwelling deep within – for submitting to His Lordship is a key to unlocking His power through our lives.

'So I say, live by the Spirit, and you will not gratify the desires of the sinful nature.'
Gal. 5:16

In fact, living by the Spirit is a lifetime pursuit so that God's holy house might be increasingly transformed.

A temple for sacrifices and a house of prayer

Being saved by grace is foundational to our faith and we heartily give thanks for what Jesus has done, but how do we then respond when He asks us to do something for Him? Are we inclined to forget who really owns this temple? It's God's, not ours, to live in as He chooses.

The purpose of the old now filters into the new, to be a temple for sacrifice and a holy house of prayer. In response to His love, therefore, we are urged to offer our bodies as living sacrifices, holy and pleasing to God, so that we may lift up holy hands in prayer (Rom. 12:1; 1 Tim. 2:8) – and the less there is of 'self' ruling the roost, the greater the capacity for God's Spirit to fill His house.

In writing this book, it is my heartfelt desire that you will join me on a journey of transformation, a path that chooses to honour the One who lives within His temple, that we all 'may be filled to the measure of all the fulness of God' (Eph. 3:19).

'And the priests could not perform their service because of the cloud, for the glory of the LORD filled his temple.'
1 Kings 8:11

Selah

During my visit to Hong Kong and India I saw a number of temples – ornate, fragrant, turreted or domed structures, built in honour of many gods such as Buddha, Brahma, Allah, Vishnu and Shiva. Owing to physical similarities, I could not always tell from their outward appearance which god they actually honoured. Only by observing the style and service of their priests, or the images and names carved on exterior walls, could I ascertain who it was they revered.

Your life was made in the image of God (Gen. 1:27), uniquely created in the womb in honour of Yahweh. From birth you've had the potential to be a temple for His Holy Spirit.

Reflect honestly on your life for a moment. Look upon it as an outsider would – not just at Sunday services but throughout 24 hours a day, seven days a week. Who or what would they perceive is being honoured and esteemed through your lifestyle, worship, service, behaviour, relationships, loyalty, conversation, passions and so on? Who or what carves their image or name on your exterior façade?

Furthermore, who or what does God see glorified when He looks beyond the walls into your heart?

If all is not as it should be, join me in finding out how to love and honour God with your heart, mind, soul and strength; your body, life and being.

'I pray, dear God, that out of Your glorious riches You may strengthen me with power through Your Spirit in my inner being, so that Christ may dwell in my heart through faith. And I pray that as I am rooted and established in love, I may have power, together with all the saints, to grasp how wide and long and high and deep is the love of Christ, and to know this love that surpasses knowledge – that I may be filled to the measure with all Your fulness.

'Now to Him who is able to do immeasurably more than all I ask or imagine, according to His power that is at work within me, to God be glory in the church and in Christ Jesus throughout all generations, for ever and ever! Amen.' (personalised from Eph. 3:16–21)

Journal

'Do you not know that your body is a temple of the Holy Spirit, who is in you, whom you have received from God? You are not your own; you were bought at a price. Therefore honour God with your body.' (1 Cor. 6:19–20)

PART TWO

A TEMPLE FOR TODAY

3 SITE UNDER CONSTRUCTION

'Then David said, "The house of the LORD God is to be here, and also the altar of burnt offering for Israel." ' (1 Chron. 22:1)

The Tale of the Temple

- When King David took a census he did evil in the eyes of God, as a result of which he was drawn to a plateau on Mount Moriah, used as a threshing-floor by Araunah the Jebusite (1 Chron. 21:7–14; 18–19). David sought God's mercy, building an altar to sacrifice burnt offerings and fellowship offerings (1 Chron. 21:25–26).
- Consequently, he realised that this threshing-floor turned place of prayer and sacrifice was, in fact, the very site God had chosen to build His holy dwelling among people (1 Chron. 22:1).

Temple for Today

'You will guide them to your holy dwelling …'

'In your unfailing love … you will guide them to your holy dwelling … You will bring them in and plant them on the mountain of your inheritance – the place, O LORD, you made for your dwelling, the sanctuary, O LORD, your hands established.'
Exod. 15:13, 17

The following free adaptation of a significant event in David's life is based on 1 Chronicles 21–22:1 and 2 Samuel 24. The scene is set at Mount Moriah, Jerusalem; the date is *circa* 990 BC.

A double-edged sword extended over Jerusalem on the brink of slaughter, scattering sunlit reflections from its burnished blade. With a keen but weary eye, David fearfully traced the ominous length to its gleaming hilt – desperately aware this was no mere trick of his troubled imagination. Indeed, a translucent body shimmered high above the city, its face masked by the brilliance of fiery darts emanating from its head and shoulders; its immense hand glued to the hilt of that awesome sword.

Overwhelmed, David fell, face-down to the ground. Sweat congealed with dirt on his brow as trembling fingers scratched at the earth, scrabbling for an impossible answer to his dilemma. Distress consumed him, his conscience lacerated with guilt. The catastrophic plague was entirely his fault owing to his self-sufficiency; even his most trusted commanders had tried to dissuade him from taking a census but were overruled by his stubborn pride. His mind tumbled in the confusion of 'what if's?', 'what now's?' and 'if only's', anguished cries escaping his mental turmoil.

'Oh God, it's not their fault. They've done nothing wrong but to follow my vain command. Take out Your wrath on me and my family but have mercy and remove this plague from Your innocent people.'

For how long he lay on the ground with his elders he could not recall, when footsteps approached him, knees bent beside him and the familiar hand of Gad, his trusted seer, raised his chin from the floor. 'My lord and my king, go up Mount Moriah until you find the threshing-floor of Araunah the Jebusite. There build an altar to the Lord,' Gad instructed with prophetic authority.

In stunned silence David hauled himself up and, without further question, traipsed up the mountainside.

Meanwhile, Araunah, a native of those parts, whose Jebusite ancestors lived in Canaan long before the Israelite invasion, had been working since dawn. Fluffy, white clouds scuttled across deep blue skies as warming trade-winds breezed in upon the raised plateau, high up Mount Moriah. The day heralded perfect weather for threshing and winnowing the recent wheat harvest lying in sheaves almost knee-deep across the threshing-floor. Araunah appreciated the rest from back-breaking sickle work as he gently guided the oxen over the sheaves, their stone-studded sledges making light work of loosening stalks from grain. He mused at his sons who followed behind, laughing and chattering, dreaming and planning as they tossed the wheat with long, pronged forks.

Without warning, the wind died, an unearthly stillness encompassing the plateau as the boys' voices trailed away, their forks abandoned in the straw. Araunah turned to scold them but gaped in fear at the iridescent warrior towering above him, a hefty sword poised right over his head.

Shortly after, King David approached and Araunah crumpled to the floor.

'My lord, and my king!' he said. 'How can I be of humble service?'

'Let me buy your threshing-floor,' David answered. 'Sell it to me for the full price so that I may seek the Lord's mercy in building Him an altar.'

Araunah's relief tumbled out in response, 'Take it! Take the whole lot. You'll need the oxen for the burnt offerings, and here are the threshing-sledges and ox-yokes for wood. Here, take my wheat too, for the grain offering. Take what you need, my king, that the Lord your God may accept you.'

But David refused to take even one grain of wheat without making payment, for he would not sacrifice a burnt offering that had not cost him anything. And so he paid Araunah the full price for his threshing-floor and equipment, and immediately set to building an altar of stone. He used the wood for kindling, slaughtered the oxen and then sacrificed burnt offerings and fellowship offerings on that Mount Moriah plateau. Lying prostrate, he called on the Lord, and the Lord sent fire from heaven onto the altar.

The mighty sword whistled across the plateau to be replaced in its sheath, but a long while passed before David arose from beside the dying embers.

'Surely,' he declared to the silent night, 'the house of the Lord God is to be here, with the altar of burnt offering for Israel.'

Contract of conversion: handing over the rights

I'm intrigued by the fact that for reasons of forgiving sin and delivering the Israelites from calamity, God led David to the spot where He'd chosen to live among His people. David insisted on paying Araunah the full price for his Mount Moriah threshing-floor and, in so doing, he purchased complete authority over Araunah's previous livelihood; authorisation to break up and burn the old equipment and take charge over future use and construction of the site. Sound familiar?

'… for all have sinned and fall short of the glory of God, and are justified freely by his grace through the redemption that came by Christ Jesus.'
Rom. 3:23–24

David wasn't the only one to sin; we've all joined him, and the penalty of death and destruction hasn't changed. But Jesus paid the highest price possible to purchase our lives as a site for God's temple – a ready-made framework awaiting our invitation to allow Him within.

Our conversion encompasses both David then Araunah's Mount Moriah experience. Like David, we may have had an awareness of impending death as a result of our sins, the confession of our wrongdoings, a desperate need for God's mercy and a turning of our hearts to the One who can save us. And like Araunah, we may have known the subsequent submission of our lives to their rightful owner, to our King who made full payment. But to what extent are we allowing God to transform the prospective site of our lives into His holy dwelling-place? Are we letting Him do it His way or do we still drag around some of our old familiar 'yokes'? Have we surrendered the complete ownership rights to Him or do we just invite Him on site when it suits us? Although we are grateful for what He has done, are we inclined to work as tenant-manager, using our own discretion on how best to use the property?

'You are not your own; you were bought at a price.'
1 Cor. 6:19–20

Site for consecration

God chose us and created us to be a living temple in which He can live by His Spirit but what have we been doing, in and to this body of ours, since first being aware it was the site of God's residence – 10 days, 10 months, 10, 40, 80 years ago …? God's holy temple was built upon a place of threshing, winnowing and sifting the chaff from the grain. Have we allowed Him to sift the chaff from our lives, to transform our empty shell into His consecrated dwelling-place?

'For he chose us in him before the creation of the world to be holy and blameless in his sight.'
Eph. 1:4

It's a lifetime work – turning out the old, rebuilding that which is damaged, renewing and consecrating every area in compliance with God's instructions: to be a temple for sacrifice and a holy house of prayer.

Selah

Jesus walks across the plateau of your life with winnowing fork in hand, separating the chaff from the grain. What worthless debris of your old life is He tossing into the wind? What seeds of potential for the future are now falling at His feet?

He stops and sits with you awhile, surveying the scene. What do you see – a brand-new construction site waiting for the builders; a neglected, rundown eyesore of derelict buildings; a quick-fix, shoddy makeover; or a golden, incense-filled sanctuary?

No matter what stage you're at now, ask Him to show you which rights to the site you've not yet signed over, which keys to locked doors you've not permitted Him to use; then pass them all back into the hands of their rightful owner.

Lord Jesus, thank You for paying the ultimate cost to pay the price for my life. I thank You that by faith I can sign over the rights and hand You all the keys, but realise this is only the first step of a lifelong journey. I know there will be times when I'm tempted to chase after chaff and bolt certain doors, but I ask and I trust You to work with me in a most gentle, timely and perfectly loving way as You transform my life into a suitable dwelling-place for the Holy Spirit, Amen.

4 THE ALTAR OF BURNT OFFERING

'He made a bronze altar twenty cubits long, twenty cubits wide and ten cubits high.' (2 Chron. 4:1)

The Tale of the Temple

- Both David and Zerubbabel constructed the altar of burnt offering prior to any building or restoration work on the temple itself (1 Chron. 21:22–22:1; Ezra 3:1–6).
- The altar of burnt offering was situated between the Court of Israel and the entrance to the sanctuary, reiterating the requirement for sacrifice before the priests could approach God's presence (Exod. 40:29).
- It is also known as the 'great altar' owing to its size; or the 'bronze or brazen altar' as the earlier wooden structures were overlaid with a heat-protective bronze casing; or the 'horned altar' due to the horns (or funnels) at the corners, into which were poured the drink offerings.
- In Solomon's Temple it measured 9m square and 4.5m high (2 Chron. 4:1). In the Second and Third Temples it was made of whole stones, the latter measuring 14.5m square, with a ramp leading up to a dais that provided a circuit around which the priests could present and tend the offerings.[2]
- Various sacrifices were presented upon it but its name arose from the 'burnt offering'.

Temple for Today

First things first

Most building and renovation projects begin with an overview of the plans, the collation of resources and the laying of foundations, but the very first command concerning the site of God's temple (and its later successor), was the instruction to build an altar for sacrifices.

'David built an altar to the LORD there and sacrificed burnt offerings and fellowship offerings' (1 Chron. 21:26). It became known primarily as the altar of burnt offering – the only sacrifice instituted in Mosaic Law that was totally consumed, symbolising a person's complete surrender and devotion to Yahweh. This is the altar God wants us to build on the site of His living temple, that which denotes our relinquished will arising from our commitment. But complete surrender doesn't mean 'just the parts I want to ... when I feel like it ... when it's convenient ... or when life is going well'. The devotion symbolised by the altar of burnt offering expresses a yielding of ourselves, our choices, lifestyle, work, ministries and so on, entirely to God's will. And who better to teach us how to do that than the Son of God Himself.

'Then the angel of the LORD ordered Gad to tell David to go up and build an altar to the LORD on the threshing-floor of Araunah the Jebusite.'
1 Chron. 21:18

The altar of choice

In the Garden of Gethsemane, Jesus effectively sacrificed His personal choice in preference for God's way of salvation, offering that sacrifice on the altar of a wooden cross. He was the perfect sacrifice 'once for all', doing away with the old system but continuing to challenge us with His use of metaphor: 'If anyone would come after me, he must deny himself and take up his cross daily and follow me ... And anyone who does not carry his cross and follow me cannot be my disciple' (Luke 9:23; 14:27).

Taking up the cross, for the majority of us, is not meant literally but symbolically as a conscious decision to choose God's will in preference to our own. 'Choice' in effect is, therefore, the altar of burnt offering in our living temple; the 'cross' with which we crucify

'For I have come down from heaven not to do my will but to do the will of him who sent me.'
John 6:38

'He sacrificed for their sins once for all when he offered himself.'
Heb 7:27

self. As 'self' is a living sacrifice we must take its life each morning – taking up our cross and carrying it, as it were, out of the city with the Roman soldiers and up the hill to be crucified. Self-denial is death to self, but it remains our choice to sacrifice it.

Every principle discussed in the ensuing chapters depends upon that choice. If 'self' fills the house then there's little room for God, but in tying self to the altar of choice and sacrificing it to His will, the door is opened for the Holy Spirit to flood right through. God gave us the gift of choice so that our love for Him would be heartfelt and sincere – not simply manufactured off a conveyor belt of pre-programmed clones. Sadly, however, gifts aren't always appreciated or valued, and from Adam and Eve to this day, 'choice' continues to honour or debase God's house, to make or break relationship.

Building the altar

'Father, if you are willing, take this cup from me; yet not my will, but yours be done.' Luke 22:42

Hungry and alone in the wilderness, Jesus was tempted to abuse the gift of choice for personal gratification; He was pressurised in daily life to submit that gift of choice to the crowds' expectations; and He battled with that gift of choice in the Garden of Gethsemane to avoid the pain of God's will. But Jesus never failed in using that freedom of choice to restore the bridge between God and humankind.

While we'll never match His perfect obedience, we can still seek to align our daily choices to the perfect will of God – how we spend our time and money, how we serve God in the home, church and workplace, how we respond to difficult people or situations and so on. Each 'right' choice dovetails into previous ones, building the altar as 'self' is sacrificed – burnt completely – crucified with Jesus. Some choices appear routine, even unimportant, but even those that we make using our God-given common sense may either build an altar or desecrate the temple. These choices run into thousands. A choice for one may prove more difficult than that same choice made by another, but it is not for us to compare. We're all unique, each of us adding our personal attributes to the dwelling-place of God here on earth.

Likewise, certain events in our lives may require a special sacrifice of choice – changing job, whether we should be married and if so to whom, forgoing the regular income of paid employment and so on. All these decisions require concerted prayer to understand the mind of God and so make the right decision, but it's the routine, daily choices that keep the fires burning.

Kindle the fire

'The fire must be kept burning on the altar continuously; it must not go out.'
Lev. 6:13

The fire on the altar was never allowed to go out and nor should ours, for as Paul says, 'Do not put out the Spirit's fire' (1 Thess. 5:19). Just as throwing a bucket of water diminishes the flames, so making self-inclined decisions and ungodly choices of attitude or response douses the Spirit's fire within. How can we prevent this from happening but by learning to please God; by choosing and submitting to His will and His ways? The more we get to know someone, the greater our knowledge of his or her likes and dislikes. The more we get to know God, the greater our likelihood of discerning His choice. Knowing 'of' or 'about' God is quite different from 'knowing' God but, by hearing His voice through prayer, the Word and His nudges upon our conscience, we can begin to make His ways our ways, His choices our choices.

So consider all the building and renovation work God has planned for your living temple. It's certainly an exciting prospect, but Scripture determines the pattern to follow: the altar must come first. Don't be tempted to skip this stage in your haste to lay down 'bricks and mortar'.

Selah

Come with me now and let's sit by Solomon's massive altar, standing outside the sanctuary of God's presence. Consider how attentive you are to the choices you make each day, for they have the power to fuel or frustrate your depth of relationship with God.

Now take each of those choices and lay them down before Him – one choice on top of another, building an altar on the site of your life. Determine now that you won't come back to remove or amend any of those decisions to suit your preferred desires, for if you shift them, the whole lot might topple over!

Alongside the knives on the tables nearby you can see some bronze utensils – pots, shovels, sprinkling bowls, meat forks and firepans used to tend the altar (Exod. 38:3). Do you use the finest tools He's given you to tend your altar of choice in an upright and godly fashion? Are you listening and submitting to, reading and obeying His gentle words to your soul – using and caring for the tools He's given you to maintain their gleaming appearance and razor-sharp edge? The coals are laid, the sacrifice is waiting, but are you willing to kindle the all-consuming fire?

Over the walls, high up on a hill, stands a lone and empty cross – a new altar for a new covenant. Self will do anything to get its own way but you have the freedom to make God's choices.

Father God, help me to see that Your choices are born out of Your great love for me, made with Your best intentions for my life. Forgive me when I prefer doing things my own way when it seems easier, quicker or much more fun. 'Show me your ways, O Lord, teach me your paths; guide me in your truth and teach me ...' Amen. (Psa. 25:4–5)

5 PREPARE AND PROVIDE

' "... I will make preparations for it." So David made extensive preparations before his death.' (1 Chron. 22:5)

The Tale of the Temple

David perceived how great and magnificent the temple would be, so he began to make extensive preparations for it on behalf of his young and inexperienced son (1 Chron. 22:5).

He went to great trouble to provide for the temple using both national and personal resources to do so (1 Chron. 22:14; 29:2–3).

In all these preliminary arrangements he prepared the resources with integrity and provided them with honest intent (1 Chron. 29:17).

Temple for Today

Having built his first altar on the site of God's temple, David wasted no time gathering people and resources to prepare for this magnificent project. He took a great deal of trouble to provide in the region of 3,775 tons of gold, 37,750 tons of silver, immeasurable quantities of bronze, iron, wood and stone, and large quantities of onyx, turquoise, colourful gemstones and marble. Furthermore, he gave freely out of his own personal wealth, approximately 113 tons of finest gold and 214 tons of silver (1 Chron. 29:1–5).

'With all my resources I have provided for the temple of my God.'
1 Chron. 29:2

Just because David was a wealthy king, however, didn't make it easy for him to resource such a vast project. He wasn't preparing for a temple that would simply display the riches he'd attained as a successful warrior, but gave the best that he could – including his personal wealth – to ensure he brought honour to God. His sacrificial personal giving was a direct result of his devotion to the Lord's temple, not wanting anything to deter from its subsequent grandeur.

'I have taken great pains to provide for the temple of the LORD ...'
1 Chron. 22:14

Ageless principles

The size of our bank account or the wealth within our jewellery box is meaningless to a temple of flesh, blood and bone. But we have faith which is of far greater worth than gold (1 Pet. 1:7), the fruit of the Holy Spirit which surpasses choice silver (Prov. 8:19) and knowledge of God's Word that is more precious than rubies (Prov. 8:10–11). Nevertheless, we can still learn from David's liberal generosity which ensured God's house should be built for 'great magnificence and fame and splendour in the sight of all the nations' (1 Chron. 22:5).

So too, in our living temple, God desires an inner beauty that is truly magnificent, a revealing of His splendour through our behaviour and lives, a testimony so powerful as to gain 'fame' and interest as it circulates among friends and further afield. Sadly, however, our fallen nature craves the attention of other people rather than God, so much so that self tingles temptingly in anticipation of all the marvellous things God might do through us. Unless, therefore, we check the motives of our hearts and the purity of our devotion at the outset, we might just find we've built ourselves a temple to house 'self' instead of God's Holy Spirit.

As David prayed earnestly at the commissioning of the project he highlighted the principles underlying all his arrangements: 'I know, my God, that you test the heart and are pleased with integrity. All these things have I given willingly and with honest intent ...' (1 Chron. 29:17). And so now it's our turn, to prepare our hearts with integrity and provide for God's temple with honest intent.

'Teacher ... we know you are a man of integrity and that you teach the way of God in accordance with the truth. You aren't swayed by men, because you pay no attention to who they are.'
Matt. 22:16

Prepare with integrity

David understood what was necessary to provide for a magnificent temple and, being a man of integrity, he simply got on with it (1 Kings 9:4). Both publicly and privately he went to great trouble to make available the resources required. He wasn't put off by the cost to himself or his country; nothing was too much to ensure God's honour was upheld within His dwelling-place.

Jesus, God's perfect tabernacle, was also a man of integrity. He never compromised with the ways of the world but adhered to God's righteousness perfectly. Jesus was authentic – His public image mirroring His private practices and inward intentions. And we too are called to a life of integrity by obeying God's commands in the small matters of life as well as the crucial decisions; giving God the best that we've got both in public and in private; choosing God's ways of holiness whatever our situation or circumstance and upholding God's name no matter whose company we are in.

Provide with honest intent

David longed for God to have a magnificent dwelling-place and so he gave towards the project the best he could provide. He wasn't trying to bribe God's approval or blessing but didn't withhold his resources to pay for his current comforts. Motivated by love and a yearning to please his God he simply intended to provide Him the best that he could. Passing his mantle on to Solomon, David reminded him that, 'the LORD searches every heart and understands every motive behind the thoughts' (1 Chron. 28:9) – a mantle God now passes on to us.

So as we reflect on renovating the temple, are we actually out to win God's favour or prove ourselves worthy of His love? He's not interested in a temple motivated to appease and promote self or any other idol but wants His dwelling-place all to Himself. That, therefore, must be the honest intention of our hearts as we seek to refurbish His sanctuary in our lives.

Whatever motivates us will energise and move us in its direction. If it's admiration from others then we'll seek to impress them; if it's personal comfort then we'll seek self-satisfaction – in fact our attitudes, behaviour, efforts and resources will be used in the main to promote that cause, even under the guise of Christian service. David's intentions, however, were completely honest, purely motivated to resource a magnificent dwelling-place for the God whom he loved, and so he provided for it as best as he was able.

'All a man's ways seem innocent to him, but motives are weighed by the LORD.'
Prov. 16:2

God's temple should influence the people among whom it resides, not vice versa! The double standard of hypocrisy, however – professing to believe one thing while practising quite the contrary – blatantly undermines our purpose and witness. God will not be mocked by fickle, half-hearted builders so let's establish from

'The integrity of the upright guides them, but the unfaithful are destroyed by their duplicity.'
Prov. 11:3

the outset our exact intention, and '... if serving the LORD seems undesirable to you, then choose for yourselves this day whom you will serve ...' (Josh. 24:15).

Likewise, motives will determine whether or not we'll put into practice our intentions concerning God's temple. Are we really motivated to house God's honour or still rather swayed by our need for self-promotion? Are we sold out to build His magnificent dwelling-place or itching to cut a slice of its glory for ourselves? David took great pains to provide for his Lord's house – the hallmark of his integrity and honest intent, authenticating the quality of his provisions. Let's follow in his footsteps.

Selah

Have you ever had 'cowboy' builders whose work is no more than a botched job – fancy façades disguising shoddy workmanship simply to earn a fast buck? It's tempting to slate their lack of integrity but have you ever considered your own approach to providing for God's temple? What's the hallmark on your provisions – cast off rubbish or the best you can provide? What's the motive in your desire to renovate God's dwelling – admiration of others or a means to honour God?

The resources to continue with the work are piled up all about you – some perhaps still wrapped within their packaging. But where are you at the moment with what you've read so far? Are you still sitting on the threshing-floor admiring the scenic view? Are you lazing in the sunshine, dozing in the grass, listening but not applying what you've heard? Are you dawdling around the building site lacking motivation to get on with the job? Are you tempted to take some short-cuts that you hope no one will notice? Or are you passionately motivated towards releasing God's glory in and through your life?

The site is cleared, the altar is under construction, but what do you really have in mind as you envisage the renovated temple? Ask God to stir up His own temple intentions in your heart, just as He did for Zerubbabel (Hag. 1:14); then take up His challenge and press on with the task.

Lord Jesus, living my life with an increased awareness of Your constant companionship will deter me from duplicity. I ask, therefore, that You would nudge me throughout the day to remind me You're still there, observing everything I do and say and wanting to help me choose Your way. 'May integrity and uprightness protect me, because my hope is in you.' Amen. (Psa. 25:21)

6 BE STRONG AND DO THE WORK

'Consider now, for the LORD has chosen you to build a temple as a sanctuary. Be strong and do the work.' (1 Chron. 28:10)

The Tale of the Temple

- Although David had the idea to build a temple to replace the tabernacle, his son was chosen for the actual task (1 Chron. 17:1–14; 22:7–8).
- Solomon was young and inexperienced but his father gave him sound advice and encouragement to help him address his responsibilities (1 Chron. 28:8–10; 29:1).
- Skilled craftsmen were employed to help the labourers with the work (1 Kings 5:6; 7:14)

Temple for Today

While reading David's story inspires me to conform to being God's holy temple, I question whether I've the necessary commitment and motivation mentioned previously to actually get on with it. Good intentions have mocked me throughout life – the intention to revise well for exams, to lose weight, to tame my tongue, to spend more time in prayer and so on. I've even read many interesting books that help and encourage these pursuits, but experience proves that being inspired by what I read is a far cry from engaging with the material and putting it into practice. Good intentions, I now realise, will be implemented only when motivated by a passion for the goal in question, but it's also very helpful to have someone nearby to encourage me along the way.

David was a man after God's own heart – he loved Him deeply, yearned to be with Him and sought His face continually (Psa. 18:1; 27:4,8). No greater force could have motivated him to provide so painstakingly for the temple, but Solomon had to take up the baton and run with it. No book or person, not even his own father could manufacture that passion on Solomon's behalf, for it had to grow within him for himself – and despite all his wealth and wisdom he was shaking in his sandals! 'But I am only a little child and do not know how to carry out my duties …' (1 Kings 3:7). David also recognised that the task was great but knew that God would be Solomon's constant companion, if only his son would seek Him as he had done. For this reason, David counselled him with three pieces of encouraging, helpful advice that can comfort and inspire us today.

'… the one whom God has chosen is young and inexperienced.'
1 Chron. 29:1

First encouragement
'Solomon your son is the one who will build my house and my courts …' (1 Chron. 28:6)

David acknowledged publicly that of all his many sons, it was Solomon whom God had chosen to build the temple. Even though David would have liked to build it, the task was for Solomon and could not therefore be delegated to anybody else.

'The one who calls you is faithful and he will do it.'
1 Thess. 5:24

No one can build a temple in my life other than me and no one can build a temple in your life other than you. We are chosen to be God's temple and as we believe in Him and invite His Spirit to reign supreme within us so the work of transformation to a holy dwelling begins, for:

> In him we were also chosen, having been predestined according to the plan of him who works out everything in conformity with the purpose of his will, in order that we … might be for the praise of his glory. (Eph. 1:11–12)

So be encouraged because God will never choose us for a task without ensuring we have everything we need to complete it, and He guarantees success provided we remain doing it in His way and His time.

Second encouragement

'Serve him with wholehearted devotion and a willing mind ...' (1 Chron. 28:9)

'Now it is required that those who have been given a trust must prove faithful.'
1 Cor. 4:2

Solomon was chosen, but his responsibility towards the project demanded wholehearted devotion to God and a willingness to obey all His instructions. We are saved by grace and God promises to equip and transform us by His Spirit, but He seeks a committed response.

This level of devotion develops from a sincere appreciation and respect for God that deepens our love to the point that we can't bear to say or do anything that would upset Him. Anytime we have a problem obeying God, however, it is probably an indication we've turned the attention onto 'I' and off 'Him'. What 'I' wants can never compare with what 'He' has done and the more we appreciate that then the more we'll long to show our gratitude.

Third encouragement

'He will not fail you or forsake you ...' (1 Chron. 28:20)

'Never will I leave you; never will I forsake you.'
Heb. 13:5

If you've ever had any building work done on your own home you may well have encountered some obstacles – delays owing to bad weather, unforeseen weaknesses in the original structure, price increases, inadequate foundations and so on. As we consider our renovations we might expect some struggles along the way, too, but God is ever present to guide us over the pitfalls, strengthen previous weaknesses and help us through the difficulties. In fact, He has promised never to leave until all the work is completed, and as that will take a lifetime we've no worries of Him abandoning the building-site halfway through construction! When we lack confidence to carry on, or sense that we've failed, let's remember the strength that He's given us to continue – the presence of His Spirit to comfort and to guide.

So be encouraged, because although we won't miraculously change overnight, the Architect has called us to partner Him in creating a suitable dwelling-place and He will not let us down.

Fourth encouragement
Skilled craftsmen

With his father's advice fresh in his mind, Solomon approached others for help, knowing that his own skills were inadequate for the task of building an exquisite temple. He knew he couldn't risk his valuable resources in unskilled hands – after all, would you let your seventeen-year-old learn to drive in your brand-new Ferrari, or set out your very best dinner service for an under-eight's birthday party?

> 'My men will work with yours ... You know that we have no-one so skilled in felling timber as the Sidonians ... Send me, therefore, a man skilled to work in gold and silver, bronze and iron, and in purple, crimson and blue yarn, and experienced in the art of engraving, to work ... with my skilled craftsmen ...' (1 Kings 5:6; 2 Chron. 2:7)

God wasn't about to stand by and watch him botch the job, so He made sure that Solomon received the help that he needed – granting him a favourable response from the neighbouring king of Tyre.

The resources we have for God's holy temple are priceless but until we hand them over to the skills of the Master Craftsman we'll risk using them incompetently in building personal monuments. As we allow the Holy Spirit to use and take control of our lives, however, we will bear fruit for God's glory that we could never harvest alone. And so He invites us to learn from and work with Him, but He must always be recognised and respected as the Supervisor of Works.

Therefore,

> Be strong and courageous, and do the work. Do not be afraid or discouraged, for the LORD God, my God, is with you. He will not fail you or forsake you until all the work for the service of the temple of the LORD is finished. (1 Chron. 28:20)

'Remain in me, and I will remain in you. No branch can bear fruit by itself; it must remain in the vine. Neither can you bear fruit unless you remain in me.'
John 15:4

Selah

God smiles affectionately upon your renewed desire to renovate a reverent, holy dwelling-place where His Spirit will feel comfortable and at home. He knows that some days will go better than others and that sometimes you may even take steps backwards but He longs to encourage you in your tasks. He will never leave you or forsake you and will remain right there with you – partnering, equipping, strengthening and inspiring you to persevere. You are not, and never will be, alone.

Ask the Holy Spirit to overrule as Master Craftsman in every area of your life; listen to what He's saying and watch what He's doing. Rely on His skills to teach you how to develop your faith and how to nurture every facet of your life as an act of worship and service to God.

Father God, my spirit is willing but my body is weak; my heart is sincere but my will is faulty. Thank You that You pick me up each time I fail and fall and use the little I can offer to build an awesome sanctuary. Please guide me step by step, stone by stone, nugget by nugget into all that You have planned and purposed for my life, Amen.

7 THE ARCHITECT'S PLANS

' "All this," David said, "I have in writing from the hand of the LORD upon me, and he gave me understanding in all the details of the plan." ' (1 Chron. 28:19)

The Tale of the Temple

- Solomon built the temple in all its detail according to a plan that God gave to David (1 Kings 6:38).
- This plan included the overall design, the weight of materials to be used and details of the work of priests and Levites in temple service and ministry (1 Chron. 28:11–19).

Temple for Today

Whether or not you've any experience of building plans it goes without saying that they aren't just pretty pictures to stimulate the imagination, but have a vital part to play in construction work. In fact, the only way a builder will accomplish the desired outcome is to first consider the architect's plans. And even after that preliminary overview, he will need to refer back to them throughout construction, checking each detail to ensure size, proportion, perspective and material are maintained as the designer intended.

'Unless the LORD builds the house, its builders labour in vain.'
Psa. 127:1

So, I wonder how different the temple would have looked if it had been built to a human plan rather than God's? I wonder how different my life would be if it were lived in accord with God's design rather than my own aspirations?

... all the details of the plan ...

'He gave him the plans of all that the Spirit had put in his mind ...'
1 Chron. 28:12

God always has a plan with user-friendly instructions to help those He chooses to do His work. He gave Noah detailed instructions on how to build the ark (Gen. 6:11–22), He told Moses exactly how the tabernacle should be constructed (Exod. 26–30) and by His Spirit put on David's mind all the plans for the temple. They weren't just artist's impressions allowing scope for human interpretation, but finely detailed instructions regarding architecture, ministry and furnishings, and they are just as comprehensive today.

'For you created my inmost being; you knit me together in my mother's womb. I praise you because I am fearfully and wonderfully made ... All the days ordained for me were written in your book before one of them came to be.'
Psa. 139:13–14,16

God designed a unique, all-encompassing life-plan when He created us concerning every single aspect of who we are – the blueprint of divine potential for our physique, personality, talents and so on. But believing in a plan doesn't automatically imply that we follow it. First we need to find out what it is; then guard against failing to adhere to it.

Do we know God's plan?

David was sufficiently focused on God to be highly attuned to receive and understand His plans in all their detail without any need for guesswork. Likewise, as we seek God with all our heart He will reveal His plans concerning the architecture – our physical body; the ministry – our service; and the furnishings – our temperament, mentality, talents and so on. It takes personal discipline and complete trust in God to apply His instructions 'in all their detail' but it's our responsibility to do so. The more we seek Him, the clearer His plans will become and the greater the likelihood we'll put them into practice in preference to our own. And as ours is a living temple whose plan will take a lifetime to complete, it compels us to keep in constant touch with the divine drawing board.

'For I know the plans I have for you ... plans to prosper you and not to harm you, plans to give you hope and a future ... You will seek me and find me when you seek me with all your heart.'
Jer. 29:11,13

But are we hearing God clearly or do we lack time and concentration to check out the finer components? And even when we do hear, are we tempted to adapt His instructions to suit our personal preference, convenience or confidence levels, so overruling His infinite knowledge and purpose with our limited perspective and understanding?

I hope this book will encourage us all to seek God's plan for temple ministry and furnishings, instructions that will continue to unfold throughout each day of our lives. But for now let's consider how His architectural details apply to our unique bodies.

The architectural blueprint

Our Father is proud of His living temple and gazes lovingly upon His exclusive handiwork, but how do we feel about it? Have we accepted His design or hankered after a different one? Have we cherished our unique frame or coveted a physique that fits the fickle preference of today's society? Who dictates to us what is right or wrong, good or bad – health gurus, fitness fanatics or supermodels who are simply mere men and women; or our loving Father God who designed us in the first place?

Sadly, we live in a world where accident and disease cause all kinds of damage to the temple structure. From the moment of conception our physical being is vulnerable to the fallen world and at one point or another develops varying degrees of problems. Sometimes God chooses to intervene and repair the damage, but He also asks many to live in their broken bodies for reasons far higher than our limited understanding. Many suffering Christians exhibit far sweeter grace than healthier ones but it would be trite and incorrect to claim that's why God hasn't healed them. However marred our frame may be, God continues to love each one of His dwellings with equal passion. The purpose of His plan for us cannot be touched by the fallen world and remains intact for all who seek to know what it is.

In contrast to worldly priorities our bodies are by no means the most important part of His residence. After all, they are only temporary whereas that which they contain will live on for eternity. We have a responsibility to care for them which we'll consider in the next chapter, but let's not forget that it was God's great pleasure to design them in conjunction with every aspect of our lives before one of our days came to be.

We have the power and potential within us to align ourselves to God's plan for our lives simply because He is in residence, so let's tap in and make use of it. Let's pause once again to 'fix our eyes on Jesus, the author and perfecter of our faith' (Heb. 12:2). He holds out the plans that were perfectly designed for each one of us and waits patiently for us to adhere to them.

Selah

Can you picture Jesus in front of His drawing board? It's a blueprint for your life, detailing every inch of your spiritual, mental and emotional being. He's beckoning you over to take a look but are you too busy or too afraid of what His plans might require of you, embarrassed perhaps by what others might think if you followed them? Fear and embarrassment of following His will may arise from a sense of inadequacy – unsure that you'll succeed or meet the expectations of others. But if you choose to ignore certain details, or adapt them to your personal preference, you'll run the risk of missing out on the higher things God has planned for you. Remember, therefore, that He created the design-plan long before you were even born and longs for you to work alongside Him in realising its potential … and it's never too late to begin!

Now take a look at its pre-prepared architecture. Like clay in the potter's hands God took you in His own hands and shaped you just as He intended. 'Shall what is formed say to him who formed it, "He did not make me"? Can the pot say of the potter, "He knows nothing"?' (Isa. 29:16). The Potter lovingly moulded the clay so please don't try and squeeze it into someone else's mould.

In this quiet moment, Lord, tell me which area I've added to this temple which is not actually a part of Your plan ...

... and also if there's anything in Your design that I've failed to notice through being too busy or being too afraid of the possible consequences upon my current lifestyle.

As for my physical framework, please help me to accept and love it just as You do – and to know and rely on Your strength where it's weak and broken, Amen.

8 THE BUILDING BLOCKS OF LIFE

' "Give careful thought to your ways. Go up into the mountains and bring down timber and build the house, so that I may take pleasure in it and be honoured," says the Lord.*' (Hag. 1:7–8)*

The Tale of the Temple

- The provisions for building and subsequent ministry included quality stone, various types of wood, iron, bronze, marble, gold, silver, gemstones, fine linen and yarn (1 Chron. 22:14; 2 Chron. 2:7–8). These materials were of the finest quality available to David and Solomon at the time.
- For example, Cedars of Lebanon were the prized timber sought out from Israel's neighbour (1 Kings 5:6).
- Nor did they make do with just any old rocks but rather large blocks of quality stone, dressed at the quarry (1 Kings 5:17; 6:7). Some of the blocks excavated from Herod's Temple are simply colossal, measuring 6–12m long, weighing over 100,000kg![3]
- Although there is some dispute as to the locations of Ophir (1 Chron. 29:4) and Parvaim (2 Chron. 3:6), which may be located in Arabia, they would not have taken the trouble to import this gold had it not been the finest available (1 Kings 6:20–21). Similarly, only refined silver was considered worthy of God's holy house.

Temple for Today

God's creative power began to build the framework of His living temple from the moment we were conceived – hewn, as it were, from the quarry of our parents' gene pool. It was handed back to its rightful owner from the moment of our Christian conversion and while we must accept His overall design it remains our responsibility to take care of its ongoing maintenance.

Most of our reflections in this book focus on our inward being and worship; after all, the outer framework of the temple is a temporary tent, limited to our time allocated in the world. For this reason, it's important that we don't prolong our outward contemplations but nevertheless take sufficient time to appreciate our duties concerning its upkeep.

Quality stone and marble; prized, majestic cedar; pure, finest gold

Solomon, Zerubbabel and Herod built for the King of kings with the finest materials available to them in the tenth, sixth and first centuries BC respectively. Zerubbabel's was far less magnificent than the others but he did the best he could do at that time. Here is our guide for maintaining our physical bodies as best possible, in the country where we live and with the resources available in twenty-first century AD.

Eating and drinking the foods on offer nowadays is a far cry from the natural, uncontaminated resources originally provided. From the paradise plants and fruits of Eden and the offspring of Noah's furry and feathered friends, to Abraham's curds and Canaan's gigantic grapes, our ancestors enjoyed unpolluted natural foodstuffs, just as God intended. So what happened?

'Everything that lives and moves will be food for you. Just as I gave you the green plants, I now give you everything.' Gen. 9:3

Culture and society have changed considerably through the ages but some would agree that our perceived 'culinary advancements' have gone just a little too far from the wholesome materials intended to strengthen our vulnerable frame. Would God even recognise some of the modern concoctions we disguise with a label called 'food'? Gone are the days when we hunted for meat, caught our fish, foraged for fruit, grew all our vegetables and popped outdoors to milk the goat! Sadly, the advantages of supermarket shopping disguise the disadvantages that make it possible – so many chemical additions and harmful processes undergone by the foodstuffs that appear so fresh and innocent-looking beneath their hygienic, cellophane wrappings.

Nevertheless, God appointed us to live, work and engage with the twenty-first century, pollution and convenience foods included. I'm not promoting food fanaticism but I am suggesting that what and how much we put in our mouths can build up or damage, please or grieve, honour or scorn the temple of the One we call Lord.

The rage of the age

Despite the extent of adulterated food on offer, promoting a healthy diet is the rage of the age but we need to define its purpose. Some may be tempted to eat unhealthily when it's quicker or more convenient or to satisfy fleshly appetites. Others get so engrossed by what they eat that diet and body shape become their idols.

A healthy balanced diet, however, can be one of the ways we honour God with our physical body by using the best building blocks available. We've a framework of bone, a covering of skin, a host of organs and tissues and a life-supporting blood supply, all of which can be built up or damaged depending on how we nourish them.

'From this day on … give careful thought to the day when the foundation of the L*ORD's temple was laid. Give careful thought …'*
Hag. 2:18

We'll never find a Bible verse condemning convenience foods or sugar-laced fat-filled treats as they didn't exist when it was written, but Scripture does teach that how we treat our body is a God-given responsibility in which at all times we must seek to please Him. Jesus partook of feasts and even turned water into wine – God's seal of approval on the tangible pleasures He created for us to enjoy. But Scripture denounces the excessive indulgence of any physical appetite, whether sex, drink or food; highlighting our choice to please and honour God or satisfy our craving. Sex is necessary for procreation but only within the confines of marriage (1 Cor. 6:18). Alcohol has been drunk since the days of Noah but drunkenness belongs to the sinful nature (Gal. 5:19–21). Food is necessary for survival but gluttony is condemned as idolatry (Col. 3:5).

' "Everything is permissible for me" – but not everything is beneficial. "Everything is permissible for me" – but I will not be mastered by anything.'
1 Cor. 6:12

Solomon could have used poor-quality stone, excess cedar wood or the wrong type of metals but in addition to using the best resources available he used the right balance of materials in accordance with God's instructions (1 Chron. 28:11–18). Likewise, therefore, '...whether you eat or drink or whatever you do, do it all for the glory of God' (1 Cor. 10:31).

Outward or inward?

Ultimately we shall each be accountable to God for what we have done in His temple – physically, as well as spiritually, mentally and emotionally. We'll never achieve a perfect diet but God asks us to give careful thought to the building blocks used to nurture and maintain His dwelling-place.

'For we must all appear before the judgment seat of Christ, that each one may receive what is due to him for the things done while in the body, whether good or bad.'
2 Cor. 5:10

No matter the strength of our cravings, our desire to be a certain size or a need to adhere to personal expectations, the true purpose of our diet is to strengthen, support and maintain the temple framework to the best of our ability – and that will depend upon where we live, the quality of air and water in our food-growing regions, and even the amount of money we can budget for it.

'Blessed are you, O land whose king is of noble birth and whose princes eat at a proper time – for strength and not for drunkenness.'
Eccl. 10:17

But to conclude this chapter in the same vein as we began, let's remember Paul's advice to Timothy, that '... physical training is of some value, but godliness has value for all things, holding promise for both the present life and the life to come' (1 Tim. 4:8). The control and maintenance of our fleshly appetites is important for a healthy framework but in renovating our inward being by the power of His Spirit we shall in fact find the strength and motivation to control the outward flesh. Indeed, godliness, revealing the ways of the One who dwells within, promises to strengthen us for today and provide hope for every tomorrow.

Selah

Consider now the meals and snacks that you've eaten these past seven days. If and when you gave thanks in prayer before a meal, could you sincerely ask God to use the food set before you to bless – that is, to nourish, build up, hone and polish – the building blocks of His living temple?

' "Food for the stomach and the stomach for food" – but God will destroy them both' (1 Cor. 6:13). Ask the Lord to help you keep the right perspective between the outer and inner being for, just as microwaves cook from the inside out, so Christ-control of the inward being reaps disciplined control of the flesh.

Thank You, Lord, for reminding me that it's not what I put into my mouth that makes me 'unclean', but rather what comes out of it. Nevertheless, as I submit to your Spirit to transform my inner being I commit myself to the responsibility of nourishing this framework You so graciously live within, Amen.

9 LAYING A FIRM FOUNDATION

'At the king's command they removed from the quarry large blocks of quality stone to provide a foundation of dressed stone for the temple.' (1 Kings 5:17)

The Tale of the Temple

- Solomon had 80,000 stonecutters in the hills of Lebanon who quarried large blocks of quality stone for the temple foundations ...
- ... The craftsmen of both Solomon and Hiram (King of Tyre) and some men from the region of Gebal then prepared the foundation of dressed stone (1 Kings 5:18).
- It was laid, measuring approximately 27m long and 9m wide (2 Chron. 3:3).
- Herod's Temple was built on a foundation of enormous solid blocks of white marble covered with gold. It was larger than Solomon's, measuring approximately 36m long and 27m wide (excluding the projections of the porch).[4]

Temple for Today

Unseen essentials

The last thing that comes to mind as I gaze upon the splendid architecture of certain museums, townhouses, towers and palaces is the key to the longevity of any building – the unseen foundations. Their design varies quite considerably depending upon the nature of the soil, the strength of the underlying rock, the magnitude of the structure to be built, the level of the water table and any history of earthquake activity. Ultimately, however, the final design must incorporate a sound structure made of quality material set into solid bedrock.

Solomon quarried quality stone to serve this immense yet unseen function in supporting the subsequent temple and it would be unwise to progress any further with our work 'above ground' before we too have checked our foundations, the bedrock on which we stand.

'There is no-one holy like the LORD; there is no-one besides you; there is no Rock like our God.'
1 Sam. 2:2

The finest bedrock

Whether we're like Solomon, building a foundation for the very first time, or Zerubbabel, rebuilding upon the originals, it's vital to ensure the base can adequately support the impending temple. Foundations need to be built into solid bedrock and ours is Jesus Christ.

If we've any uncertainty that Jesus, the Son of God, was born of a virgin, lived a perfect life, offered an all-time sacrifice for our sins, conquered death and was raised in exaltation over every living thing, then it may be time to reassess the rock on which we're attempting to build. This book is by no means the place to answer your uncertainties but I do encourage you to approach your pastor or a mature Christian friend to talk and pray through any hesitation to your belief that Jesus is the one and only way to salvation.

'... each one should be careful how he builds. For no-one can lay any foundation other than the one already laid, which is Jesus Christ.'
1 Cor. 3:10–11

It's good to have questions as it grounds our faith. Questions, however, need to be answered, either specifically, or in such a way as to stimulate faith in the unfathomable ways, the higher thoughts and the deeper understanding of Almighty God, so infinitely far beyond the parameters of our mortal intellect.

'As the heavens are higher than the earth, so are my ways higher than your ways and my thoughts than your thoughts.'
Isa. 55:9

Laying a firm foundation

The beginning of Hebrews 6 provides a succinct overview of what the Early Church considered to be the foundations of Christian faith. It was written to encourage the believers to press on from these foundations to spiritual maturity but is also a useful guide for today when the opposite can be a problem.

This may happen when adult converts who've missed out on Sunday school, youth groups, nurture groups, discipleship courses or one-to-one spiritual guidance find themselves sitting in the Sunday service being encouraged to press on to spiritual maturity without having a firm foundation on which to build. Let's take a few moments, therefore, to double-check our foundations have the strength and quality to support the wonderful sanctuary God wants to build upon them.

If we're tempted to omit this stage then remember Jesus' warning: when the rain comes and the winds blow, houses built on sand fall to the ground with a great crash (Matt. 7:24–27)!

Faith's foundations based on Hebrews 6:1–2

'... repentance from acts that lead to death ...'

I know a kind and generous old gentleman who believes his life of good works will earn him a place in heaven. Sadly, he refuses to accept that, without faith, our works cannot unlock the doors of heaven in this life or the next; 'For it is by grace you have been saved, through faith – and this not from yourselves, it is the gift of God – not by works, so that no-one can boast' (Eph. 2:8–9).

The first foundation relies on our confession that Jesus is the only way to the Father and our repentance from any lifestyle or attitude that contradicts it.

'... faith in God ...'

God's very nature is love; He is forgiving, faithful, compassionate, all-powerful, merciful, and so much more (1 John 4:8; Psa. 130:3–4; 89:8). His love guarantees unconditional acceptance, His mercy offers unquestionable forgiveness and His faithfulness provides absolute security for all life's ups and downs.

This foundation reminds us to put our faith in God for who He is, what He has done and what He'll continue to do.

'... baptisms ...'

Baptism, included in Jesus' final commission to the disciples, is the outward, personal confession or witness to our inward repentance and faith (Matt. 28:19). In being baptised we symbolise our death to self and the law of sin and death, so proclaiming that Jesus is Lord and that one day we'll share in His resurrection life.

Differing denominations perform baptism in a variety of ways but that doesn't diminish its importance.

'... laying on of hands ...'

Laying our hands on someone in prayer has nothing to do with our own abilities or perceived *spirituality* but everything to do with the One who lives within us.

Paul was no magician but the physical expression of his prayerful intent symbolised faith in God to touch the person on whom he laid hands; whether for healing, anointing or in God's chosen way (Acts 28:8; 1 Tim. 4:14).

'... the resurrection of the dead ...'

Few people deny the existence of a great teacher about 2,000 years ago but, without believing in His resurrection, His teachings amount to little more than yet another philosophy of life (1 Cor. 15:13–14).

If Jesus Christ is to have any impact upon our lives both now and for eternity then we have to believe in His resurrection – His victory over death that enables us to be raised with Him at the end of time.

'... eternal judgment ...'

As we believe in the resurrection so we must also believe in judgment, for at the end of time we shall all be called to account (Rom. 14:10–12). If we have denied Christ as Lord in this life He will deny us in the next, judging us for eternity as unworthy of His kingdom.

Sheep or goat, believer or unbeliever – we are either one or the other but we cannot try to be both.

Friends of ours were hoping to renovate and extend their town house but surveys confirmed it lacked any foundations as it stood precariously on sandstone. Builders were therefore conscripted to underpin the house to procure its safety and longevity, only after which could they then commence with the renovations and extensions.

But what underpinning do our lives need to take the weight of any extra building work? Weak foundations are first evidenced through cracks in the walls and subsequent crumbling – so let's not take any risks with our beliefs that support God's living temple!

Selah

Consider each foundation stone, one at a time. As you affirm its truth and relevance in your life, so lay it down with prayer:

1. Have you any niggling questions that in any way cause you to doubt your salvation, God's love for you, Christ's divine nature, resurrection, supremacy and so on? Who do you know that you could speak to about these things? Contact them now if you can and make an arrangement to meet up.

2. What or whom do you lean on in life? God is the only foundation that will not move, disappear, change or become faulty.

3. Have you been baptised? If not, talk to the Lord about it.

4. Laying on hands is not a formula guaranteeing the answer you would choose, but are you willing to express trust that you believe in the power of the One within you to touch the one for whom you pray, in His perfect way?

5. Do you believe that yours is not a pilgrimage to a tomb filled with bones but a pilgrimage through life to eternity because of a tomb that is empty of bones?

6. Do you accept judgment or do you try and water down its implications for non-believers?

Thank You, Lord, for these solid foundations that will stand the test of time both in this life and the next. I'm grateful for those that are already firmly in place but realise that [......] need underpinning. Please show me how to strengthen these weaknesses before I continue building, Amen.

10 THE BRONZE SEA

'He made the Sea of cast metal, circular in shape, measuring ten cubits from rim to rim and five cubits high. It took a line of thirty cubits to measure round it.' (2 Chron. 4:2)

The Tale of the Temple

- The bronze sea (or laver) was a large round tank cast from molten bronze, measuring approximately 4.5m diameter, 2m high and 13.5m circumference (2 Chron. 4:2).
- It sat on a base of 12 sculptured bulls and its rim opened out like a lily blossom. It had the capacity to hold 66 kilolitres (14.5 gallons) of water (2 Chron. 4:4–5) and probably had taps lower down on the sides for greater convenience of use.[5]
- The bronze sea was placed at the south-east corner of the Court of the Priests between the altar of burnt offering and the porch. It was used by the priests to wash and thereby consecrate themselves before ministering in the temple (2 Chron. 4:6,9–10).

Temple for Today

It's common knowledge that surgeons ought not to approach their patients without first scrubbing their hands in anti-bacterial solution, and that cooks ought not to go near any food unless they've washed their hands with soap and water. But did you know that the priests could not commence any ministry in the temple or approach God's presence in the sanctuary without washing their hands and feet?

> Then bring Aaron and his sons to the entrance to the Tent of Meeting and wash them with water … Whenever they enter the Tent of Meeting, they shall wash with water so that they will not die. Also, when they approach the altar to minister by presenting an offering made to the LORD by fire, they shall wash their hands and feet so that they will not die. (Exod. 29:4; 30:20–21)

Priestly consecration

So it was, therefore, that Solomon made a bronze sea, also known as the laver, in which priests could perform their daily ablutions before touching any sacred vessel or approaching God in prayer. Newly-ordained priests had to wash their whole bodies but those already in service merely washed their hands and feet – a symbolic act of cleansing and holy consecration, dedicating themselves formally each and every day before ministering in God's house.

Now that we are a royal priesthood (1 Pet. 2:9), God's living temple requires our worship, work and service to perform its priestly duties. At the point of our conversion we were washed completely clean by the blood of Jesus' sacrifice (1 Cor. 6:11) but daily we need to approach the bronze sea and symbolically wash our 'hands and feet' – confessing our sins and receiving forgiveness to cleanse our hearts from a guilty conscience.

'A person who has had a bath needs only to wash his feet; his whole body is clean.'
John 13:10

Jesus set us free from the law of sin and death and thankfully, therefore, from the death penalty facing priests who forgot this symbolic washing! Nevertheless, it remains a stark reminder that before we attempt to approach or serve God we ought first to visit daily our 'sea' of holy consecration through humble and heartfelt confession; to '... purify ourselves from everything that contaminates body and spirit, perfecting holiness out of reverence for God' (2 Cor. 7:1).

Cleansing through confession

Most of us feel terrible when through selfish, thoughtless, tactless or unkind words and behaviour we sadden the people we love or respect. We yearn for their forgiveness and make every effort not to hurt them in that way again. If we claim to love and revere God, therefore, how much more ought we to come and ask daily that He will forgive us for hurting Him and desecrating the temple that Jesus makes holy – for that, in a nutshell, is what sin is, grieving the Holy Spirit who lives within (Eph. 4:30).

It's important we take sufficient time here to allow the Holy Spirit to convict our conscience of both wilful and unintentional sins. Given that opportunity, He will search our hearts and bring to our minds those things that have upset Him. Nevertheless, the bronze sea was not a place for the temple priests to dwell any longer than the time it took to wash, and neither should we linger once we've offered our confession.

Sometimes, however, we find it difficult to forgive ourselves, stalling in our place of cleansing, turning over in our minds those things we've done wrong when Jesus has long since forgiven us and washed it all away. But wallowing in introspection merely distracts us from our ongoing duties in God's house. Remember, therefore, that when we sincerely repent of our wrongdoings, we can receive in full the fresh cleansing of His forgiveness without guilt or condemnation, for 'If we confess our sins, he is faithful and just and will forgive us our sins and purify us from all unrighteousness' (1 John 1:9).

'... there is now no condemnation for those who are in Christ Jesus ...'
Rom. 8:1

Be holy ...

Before too long we'll be tending the altar, climbing the steps that lead up into the sanctuary, then ministering in the courts of our lives. We recognise, therefore, that cleansing and consecration is vital to all aspects of temple ministry, for '... just as he who called you is holy, so be holy in all you do; for it is written: "Be holy, because I am holy" ' (1 Pet. 1:15–16).

In Chapter 2 we saw that Jesus makes us holy in God's sight but we have a responsibility to live a holy life, one that prevents us behaving irreverently or taking our sanctification for granted. Holiness relates to extreme purity, perfectly manifested in God – so the temple and its service had to be holy because of whom it housed. Let us live, therefore, '... in a right way in undivided devotion to the Lord' (1 Cor. 7:35), confessing our sins and submitting to His ways, not just in prayer but in practice.

'I wash my hands in innocence, and go about your altar, O LORD ... If I had cherished sin in my heart, the Lord would not have listened ...'
Psa. 26:6; 66:18

It's an active decision to 'flee' and 'avoid' all kinds of ungodly behaviour – gossip, godless chatter, filthy language, slander, criticism, complaining, sexual immorality, impurity, revelry, idolatry, witchcraft, hatred, unkindness, pride, jealousy, fits of rage, tantrums, sulks, selfish ambition, unforgiveness, arguments, drunkenness, greed and so on.

'Who may ascend the hill of the LORD? Who may stand in his holy place? He who has clean hands and a pure heart ...'
Psa. 24:3–4

We'll never be perfect, but being saved by grace we may live by the Spirit so that we will not gratify the desires of our sinful nature (Gal. 5:16). No longer being bound to legalistic laws of sin and death we are free to live a holy life by the power of God's Spirit within.

'... holiness adorns your house for endless days, O Lord.'
Psa. 93:5

Come first to the bronze sea, therefore, and determine to consecrate the day to holy ministry and service. And then '... let us draw near to God with a sincere heart in full assurance of faith, having our hearts sprinkled to cleanse us from a guilty conscience and having our bodies washed with pure water' (Heb. 10:22).

Selah

The burnished bronze of the recently filled sea is gleaming in the sunshine. Come closer and take a look at your reflection peering back from its highly polished surface. You might just be able to see your face but Jesus can see your heart – ask Him therefore to show you those things that grieve His Spirit within.

Consider how these things might have hurt Him – and then find a way of telling Him how sorry that you are.

Now open one of the taps and let that pure, cool water pour over your hands and feet – a symbol of the perfect cleansing blood of Jesus that flowed with love despite torturous pain so that you may receive God's forgiveness. Receive it and allow His mercy to pour over your soul, releasing you from guilt and condemnation.

Closing the tap, give thanks for God's unfailing grace and determine to realign your ways to His pure and holy standards, so consecrating yourself once again to His service.

'Search me, O God, and know my heart ... See if there is any offensive way in me, and lead me in the way everlasting ... Have mercy on me, O God, according to your unfailing love; according to your great compassion blot out my transgressions. Wash away all my iniquity and cleanse me from my sin ... Cleanse me with hyssop, and I shall be clean; wash me, and I shall be whiter than snow ... Hide your face from my sins and blot out all my iniquity ... Create in me a pure heart, O God, and renew a steadfast spirit within me.' Amen. (Psa. 139:23–24; 51:1–2,7,9–10)

11 LIVING SACRIFICES

'I have ... chosen this place for myself as a temple for sacrifices.' (2 Chron. 7:12)

The Tale of the Temple

Various sacrifices and offerings were presented on the altar of burnt offering, based on Mosaic Law:

- *Burnt offerings*: made at least twice daily in the temple constituting a male animal (bull, sheep or goat) without defect, or a dove or young pigeon, prepared in accordance with Mosaic Law (Lev. 1; 6:8–13) and burned up completely.
- *Grain offerings*: fine flour, with oil and incense poured over it; also fine wafers and flour cakes baked with oil, cooked over a griddle or in a pan – all without yeast but all seasoned with salt (Lev. 2; 6:14–23).
- *Fellowship offerings*: the fat and certain innards of a male or female from the herd or flock, without defect, prepared in accordance with Mosaic Law (Lev. 3; 7:11–21).
- *Sin offerings*: the fat of a young bull, goat or sheep; or two doves or pigeons; or a tenth of an ephah of fine flour, prepared in accordance with Mosaic Law (Lev. 4–5:13; 6:24–30).
- *Guilt offerings*: a ram without defect, plus appropriate restitution in accordance with Mosaic Law (Lev. 5:14–6:7; 7:1–10).

Temple for Today

On leaving our 'sea' of confession and consecration it's time to return to the altar that we built in Chapter 4; for it's not just an altar of choice that we need but a sacrifice to offer upon it. At their altar, placed right outside the sanctuary, the priests presented many daily sacrifices which flowed from dawn until dusk, starting as always with the corporate burnt offering – 'an aroma pleasing to the LORD' (Lev. 1:13).

Perhaps we don't think this is necessary now as Jesus is our all-time sin offering, but as Paul is about to remind us, we can continue offering our bodies, in fact every part of our being, as a living sacrifice.

Living sacrifices

Whether they were sin, guilt, burnt, grain or fellowship offerings, Mosaic Law provided the minutiae of instructions on how sacrifices and offerings should be slaughtered and/or presented; what to do with the blood, innards, fat and carcass; and what should be burnt completely, given to the priests or handed back to the worshipper. The plethora of rules depended on the type of person offering the sacrifice (priest, king, Israelite, foreigner, male, female and so on), the specifics of their sin, their state of Levitical 'cleanness', the type of offering and even how much a person could afford. As for the new covenant sacrifice, however, Paul simply writes: 'I urge you, brothers, in view of God's mercy, to offer your bodies as living sacrifices, holy and pleasing to God – this is your spiritual act of worship' (Rom. 12:1).

And so Paul first points out that we are offering ourselves not a bull, sheep, goat, pigeon or dove; nor even flour, wine or oil. Everything that constitutes you and me may be offered on our altar for God's good pleasure and purpose.

'I die every day – I mean that, brothers – just as surely as I glory over you in Christ Jesus our Lord.'
1 Cor. 15:31

Second, the sacrifice is living – it's an ongoing death to self; hour after hour, day after day, for the duration of years apportioned to us.

Third, it is holy – not because of what we have done, but through

Jesus' perfect sin offering; holiness that requires we align ourselves to God's standards.

Finally, it should be pleasing to God, a pleasing aroma to the Lord.

Pleasing to the Lord

What's your favourite aroma? Which smells seduce your senses – roast dinner, pungent roses, damp woodland, freshly mown grass, musty stables, mid-summer herb gardens, tomato plants, ground coffee beans, lavender sachets, baking bread …?

'… they have not listened to my words and have rejected my law … Your burnt offerings are not acceptable; your sacrifices do not please me.'
Jer. 6:19–20

Wonderful, aren't they? But these tangible pleasures rely on the physical senses while a pleasing aroma of sacrifice demands more than the smell of burning meat, for God looked beyond the visible performance to see the inward attitude; 'The sacrifices of God are a broken spirit; a broken and contrite heart …' (Psa. 51:17). Indeed, God is not fooled by mere words or religious routine. He retreats from the stench of insincere words that are never put into practice; He wrinkles His nose at a sacrifice of praise that arises from bitter hearts; He turns aside from the odour of sacrificed time that is coated in sour resentment; but He breathes in deeply the pleasing aroma of hearts that endorse prayers with action.

'Your attitude should be the same as that of Christ Jesus …'
Phil. 2:5

Jesus always did what pleased His Father (John 8:29). The last thing He wanted to face was the shame and horror of the cross but, as He hung there on our behalf, naked, bleeding and in excruciating pain, He came to the point where nothing remained that He could further offer. Jesus became nothing – He humbled Himself with complete obedience – and so, therefore, must we. But a one-off prayer of surrender at our altar will soon fade away, unless acts of submission to God's divine will continue throughout each day.

'Take your son, your only son, Isaac, whom you love, and go to the region of Moriah. Sacrifice him there as a burnt offering on one of the mountains I will tell you about.'
Gen. 22:2

Sacrifice, therefore, was and is intrinsic to temple ministry for, as Paul concludes, it is our very act of worship.

'… this is your spiritual act of worship' (Rom. 12:1)

The first mention of 'worship' appears in the life of our old friend Abraham. It occurred at the time God asked him to sacrifice the one thing he'd longed for his entire life, the son he loved with unreserved passion, the first promised evidence of God's unfolding covenant (v.5). And so it was that for three long days he travelled obediently to God's chosen place of sacrifice – a mountain at Moriah. 'Stay here …' he said to his servants, 'while I and the boy go over there. We will worship and then we will come back to you.'

Abraham's heart was right with and pleasing to God. He trusted Him implicitly despite contradictory circumstances and so he perceived the tremendous act of sacrifice as an appropriate expression of worship.

A millennium later, God led David back to Mount Moriah to present his own burnt offerings. There the people later worshipped in the glorious temple of sacrifice, and there upon that mountain Jesus gave His all – the priceless act of sacrifice, the ultimate expression of worship, prostrating Himself in complete submission to the Father's perfect will.

'… Who then am I to build a temple for him, except as a place to burn sacrifices before him?'
2 Chron. 2:6

Worship, therefore, is not merely an apportioned time in the Sunday service to sing Christian songs, declare God's praises or take up a collection for His work. Worship is the ongoing sacrificial offering of all that we are to God. He promised in His Word that He'll never forsake us and never leave us, so what have we got to lose? To give Him our all is not a risky gamble like putting your life on the stock market – rather it's the most secure, rewarding and fulfilling investment we could ever hope to make. And as a result of such trusting sacrifice there naturally flows an expression of love and adoration through prayer, music, tithing, service and so on.

In fact, the outward visible sacrifice at the altar was vital to preparing the inner core of prayer in the sanctuary. So too, as we offer ourselves in complete surrender to God, we will prepare our inward being for that intimate place of prayer.

Selah

You're standing once again at your altar and God is saying, 'Worship Me.' What is your immediate response – to open your hymn book or get out your guitar? Or, like Abraham, are you willing to tie to that altar your most treasured possessions, beloved relationships and coveted dreams?

Pause here awhile, and consider the implications of trusting God with these acts of living sacrifice, each and every day.

Father, I know that You give only the very best gifts to Your children (Matt. 7:11), which helps me to trust You completely as I now offer back on my altar everything I've perceived to be more important. I believe that Your love is far greater than this life and in faith I reach out to receive it, Amen.

12 SANCTUARY OF GOLD

'He adorned the temple with precious stones. And the gold he used was gold of Parvaim.' (2 Chron. 3:6)

The Tale of the Temple

- The Holy Place measured approximately 18m long and 9m wide with narrow clerestory windows (1 Kings 6:3,4,17).
- The walls and ceiling were panelled in cedar wood, and the floor covered with pine and the walls then carved with gourds and open flowers (1 Kings 6:9,15,18).
- Solomon covered this entire interior with fine gold, carefully hammering it evenly over the carvings then decorating it with cherubim, palm tree, chain designs, and precious stones (1 Kings 6:35; 2 Chron. 3:5–7).

Temple for Today

All the while that the lamb was being slain, priests were preparing the Holy Place in readiness for burning incense: the golden altar was cleared of its burnt coals and ash, the lamps of the golden candlesticks trimmed and refilled with oil. So join with me now and walk up the steps into this golden sanctuary; passing through the gold-plated doors to gaze upon its beauty, for 'Splendour and majesty are before him; strength and glory are in his sanctuary' (Psa. 96:6).

Daylight squeezed through narrow clerestory windows high up in the walls, scattering golden reflections into the mellow lamplight. The walls and doors were intricately carved with flowers, palm trees and cherubim, overlaid with gold then adorned with precious jewels – even the floor was carpeted with gold. Five golden lampstands and tables of showbread were laid out on either side, plus solid gold tongs, wick trimmers, sprinkling bowls, dishes and incense censers (2 Chron. 4:19–22). But its treasured possession,

'Solomon covered the inside of the temple with pure gold, and he extended gold chains across the front of the inner sanctuary, which was overlaid with gold. So he overlaid the whole interior with gold.'
1 Kings 6:21–22

the golden altar, was placed at the end of the room. It stood in front of an exquisite curtain of fine linen embroidered with blue, purple and crimson yarn with cherubim worked into it, veiling from view the Most Holy Place and the awesome glory of God (3:14). The mind boggles!

Let's pause now in this Holy Place of immediate approach to God's presence, the beautiful sanctuary that links the courts to the innermost place of His dwelling. Its dazzling beauty and immeasurable wealth entices us to draw closer; its construction and its ministry guiding our personal approach in prayer.

The golden overlay

It's no surprise that the home of our King should be suitably lavished with gold for even the dwellings of earthly royals are inevitable displays of treasure. Today, we may use it to adorn our body or fill a rotten tooth, but as for overlaying the sanctuary in our heart we need a far greater treasure – a priceless gem called faith (1 Pet. 1:7).

Faith is invaluable and cannot be stolen or destroyed. Babylonians ransacked the temple gold but faith in Almighty God is imperishable and invincible – nothing and no one can remove faith by force. Faith in itself is priceless but there are different degrees according to the level of our trust and dependency on God.

Imagine for a moment that we can measure its purity in the same way as gold – 24-carat gold is completely pure but anything less has a certain proportion of impurity mixed in with it (the proportion of gold to impurities in the 9-carat alloy is actually less than half!). If we placed 9-carat gold in a fiery furnace the impurities would separate from the valuable metal. The greater the amount of impurity removed, the higher the proportion of gold in the resultant alloy and the purer it becomes.

If we had 24-carat faith we would trust God implicitly, completely and perfectly. On the other hand, 9-carat faith acknowledges Jesus as Saviour and Lord but still relies more heavily on people or things for daily provision and purpose. Somewhere between the two we have varying degrees of dependency on God versus reliance on self, associated here to 14-, 18- or 22-carat faith.

It's interesting, therefore, how Scripture likens God to a purifier of precious metals. His ultimate design for His living temple is a sanctuary overlaid in 24-carat faith, but for that, He has to refine it!

'He will sit as a refiner and purifier of silver; he will purify the Levites and refine them like gold and silver.'
Mal. 3:3

The Refiner's fire

Jesus said if we had faith as small as a mustard seed we could move mountains and He Himself fed more than 5,000 hungry mouths with a mere five loaves and a couple of fish (Matt. 17:20; 14:15–21). As long as we give Him a nugget of faith, therefore, to line God's living sanctuary, He'll do it there and then. But just for a moment, let's recall a bereaved, bankrupt, boil-infested Job who, sitting in the dust, could still yet proclaim, '… he knows the way that I take; when he has tested me, I shall come forth as gold' (Job 23:10). His biography is one of utmost difficulty and heartache and yet his faith in God is impeccable. He believed without a shadow of doubt that the Lord still loved him and both knew and controlled events. He also trusted his suffering would someday end, at which point he would 'come forth as gold'.

> … for a little while you may have had to suffer grief in all kinds of trials. These have come so that your faith – of greater worth than gold, which perishes even though refined by fire – may be proved genuine and may result in praise, glory and honour when Jesus Christ is revealed. (1 Pet. 1:6–7)

I'm not suggesting that we'll all have to follow in Job's painful footsteps to purify our faith, but as we allow God to transform His temple He will test and refine our tainted dependency degree by degree in a furnace. If we're willing to remain with God in that furnace until the 'heat' is turned down, we'll emerge with a purer faith, lining the ever-increasing beauty of the Holy Place – whether for security in unfamiliar circumstances, the equipping for some new task, or for help and comfort through an ongoing difficult situation and so on. God will choose the time and the way in which He'll refine its purity, but let's build ourselves up in our most holy faith (Jude 20) and trust the Refiner to do His good work.

Spending time in this Holy Place of treasured faith gives space for its beauty to focus our hearts on His glory. It builds up our faith and so, in turn, our confidence to approach His presence – encouraging us towards the golden altar to touch His heart in prayer.

Selah

How are you feeling as you stand within this sanctuary – overwhelmed, unworthy, speechless ...? You may feel your faith is only small, but God has already used it to line His sanctuary. The priests had no alternative option but to approach His presence through this sanctuary of gold, but do you ever try to approach Him by works and proof of good living rather than simply through faith?

Praise God for this place of ever-increasing beauty that draws you closer to His presence, secure in the knowledge that your times – good and bad – are safe and secure in His hands (Psa. 31:15).

Lord, 'I do believe; help me overcome my unbelief!' (Mark 9:24). Thank You for revealing Yourself to my heart that I might put my faith in One whom I've never seen. Forgive me when my lack of faith hinders my approach to Your beautiful and glorious presence, Amen.

13 THE GOLDEN ALTAR OF INCENSE

'He designated the weight of gold for all the gold articles to be used in various kinds of service ... and the weight of the refined gold for the altar of incense.' (1 Chron. 28:14,18)

The Tale of the Temple

- Among other furnishings, Solomon made an altar of cedar, overlaid with gold, which was set in front of the Most Holy Place (1 Kings 6:20).
- David was given specific instructions concerning the construction and the weight of refined gold used to make it although further design details aren't actually included in the subsequent text (1 Chron. 28:18–19).
- We may, however, assume a design similar to that built in the tabernacle – approximately 0.5m long and wide, and 0.9m high, with horns extending from each corner. A gold moulding was set around the rim to prevent the coals and incense from falling off the top (Exod. 30:1–3).
- The incense burned on the altar was blended from equal quantities of fragrant spices – gum resin, onycha, galbanum and frankincense, salted then ground to a powder (Exod. 30:34–36).

Temple for Today

'Put the altar in front of the curtain ... Aaron must burn fragrant incense on the altar every morning when he tends the lamps. He must burn incense again when he lights the lamps at twilight so that incense will burn regularly before the LORD for the generations to come.'
Exod. 30:6–8

Burning incense on the golden altar was resumed twice a day – a once-in-a-lifetime priestly privilege at the morning and evening sacrifice. First filling a golden bowl with hot coals from the altar of burnt offering, the designated priest with his golden censor retired into the sanctuary.[6]

Picture the scene of this humble man a mere breath away from God's presence, arranging the coals on the golden altar as he waited in expectation. Meanwhile, outside, scores of people faced the sanctuary, falling face down – not a word, not a cough, not even a murmur as they silently spread their hands for prayer.

The incense was laid upon the golden altar, filling the Holy Place with its sweet fragrant smoke. The priests and the people began to pray, their humble worship and reverent declarations encased by the rising cloud. And so the sweet fragrance slipped through the veil, penetrating the place of God's presence.

'Once when Zechariah's division was on duty and he was serving as priest before God, he was chosen by lot, according to the custom of the priesthood, to go into the temple of the Lord and burn incense.'
Luke 1:8–9

Fragrant worship

While worshipping God with sacrificed wills results in a pleasing aroma, expressing our love with worshipping hearts exudes the fragrance of sacred incense. So, as we approach God's presence in prayer, let's take the time to revere and declare His majesty; to minister before Him with a fragrant offering of heartfelt praise. It's true that Jesus gives us access to God at any moment and for any reason so we could race right through the Holy Place, bursting headlong into His presence with a tumble of words and worries. But there are times, like the morning and evening sacrifice, when it's appropriate as priests in His living temple to focus entirely on expressing our devotion.

'Now I am about to build a temple for the Name of the LORD my God and to dedicate it to him for burning fragrant incense before him ...'
2 Chron. 2:4

One would think that God's beloved Son owned the rightful position to be unrestrained in approaching His Father and yet we learn that even His prayers were heard because of His reverent submission (Heb. 5:7). So,

> Guard your steps when you go to the house of God. Go near to listen rather than to offer the sacrifice of fools, who do not know that they

> do wrong. Do not be quick with your mouth, do not be hasty in your heart to utter anything before God. God is in heaven and you are on earth, so let your words be few. (Eccl. 5:1–2)

We still enjoy a comfortable approach to our loving Lord and Friend, but this golden sanctuary reminds us always to first revere Him as King.

Prayers like incense

Whatever God's actual reasons for choosing to burn sacred incense, it symbolised the prayerful devotion rising from priests and people. But devotion cannot be manufactured so – if we've a tendency to use empty words snatched from clichés, tradition or comfortable habit – we need to seek more meaningful ways of expressing the depth of our love and thanks. And, perhaps, to do that we simply need to develop our relationship with God, out of which our words will spontaneously flow from adoring hearts bursting with gratitude. It can be very helpful to pray psalms of praise or written forms of liturgy, but determine now to keep them fresh and avoid any stale routine formulae. We're not seeking religious rote or parrot-fashion prayer but reverent declarations from a sincere, God-seeking soul.

Prayers aren't fragrant because they're spoken out loud, with pious intonation or particular words, but simply because they sincerely seek to glorify God. Thus we come into the Holy Place to minister to our Lord with fragrant prayers born from a humble heart; coming not for what we can get but for what we can give to the One who gave everything for our sakes. Incense was burnt regularly before the Lord (Exod. 30:8); perpetually or continually as implied in its original Hebrew. Similarly, Paul asked the Colossians to 'devote' themselves to prayer (Col. 4:2) and urged the Thessalonians to 'pray continually' (1 Thess. 5:17). Nothing could be sweeter than our communion with God and to that alone we should be 'devoted' – earnest, untiring and steadfast, unperturbed by circumstance in our pursuit of seeking God's heart 'continually'.

Declaring His worth and expressing our love helps still the heart. It puts the world and its worries into perspective before God and fills His holy dwelling with the sweetness of fragrant worship.

So before we move on, let's spare a thought for Mary who, in pouring out love for Jesus as she anointed His dusty feet, filled her home with the exquisite fragrance of expensive perfume (John 12:3). It's a beautiful scene that inspires us to pour out our own loving devotion – filling our lives, God's living temple, with the fragrance of heartfelt praise: 'May my prayer be set before you like incense; may the lifting up of my hands be like the evening sacrifice' (Psa. 141:2).

Selah

Take a look around the Holy Place of your life, be inspired by its intricate carvings of faith in the deepening golden hue. Every time you approach God in prayer you may pause at the golden altar or ignore it and walk on through. It's cleaned of ash and renewed with burning coals but can you be bothered to make the effort to burn some fragrant incense – delighting His heart with the sweet sacred fragrance of devoted prayers of praise?

Take time now to use your censor and sprinkle its contents onto the golden altar. See how the rising cloud of smoke gracefully climbs towards God; and as you tell Him how much He means to you, consider how deeply He inhales its sweet fragrance.

> I, by your great mercy, will come into your house; in reverence will I bow down towards your holy temple ... Ascribe to the LORD the glory due to his name; worship the LORD in the splendour of his holiness ... Come, let us bow down in worship, let us kneel before the LORD our Maker. (Psa. 5:7; 29:2; 95:6)

Without getting bound by rigid self-made laws, how might you develop this priestly aspect of inward fragrant prayer?

Lord, I'm sorry for the times that I've merely given this altar a cursory glance or a token handful of incense without regularly spending time here to minister to You with the fragrance of prayerful worship.

Thank You that I've found a way to simply bring You pleasure – a grateful response for the immeasurable pleasures You constantly give to me, Amen.

14 THE POWER ROOM

'He built the Most Holy Place, its length corresponding to the width of the temple – twenty cubits long and twenty cubits wide ... the innermost room, the Most Holy Place ...' (2 Chron. 3:8; 1 Kings 7:50)

The Tale of the Temple

- The Most Holy Place, Holy of Holies or innermost room was about 9m long and wide, its interior overlaid with 21 metric tons of gold (2 Chron. 3:8).
- The Holy Place was separated from the Most Holy Place by a cedar-wood partition (overlaid with gold), upon which hung the intricately embroidered linen curtain of blue, purple and crimson yarn with cherubim worked into it (1 Kings 6:16; 2 Chron. 3:14).
- Solomon made two golden cherubim with wings outstretched, the tips of which touched in the middle where they met and both walls on either side. They stood, approximately 4.5m high, facing the Holy Place (1 Kings 6:23–28; 2 Chron. 3:13).
- The ark of the covenant, holding Moses' two tablets of the Law, were brought into the innermost room and positioned beneath the wings of the cherubim (2 Chron. 5:7–10).
- By Herod's day, the Most Holy Place was empty except for a large stone – the ark of the covenant and the cherubim having long since disappeared.[7]

Temple for Today

On the tenth day of Tishri (the Hebrew month falling between mid-September and mid-October), the high priest passed beyond the brightly embroidered curtain into the innermost room of the sanctuary. Only one man, once a year, had the esteemed permission to walk beyond the veil on that annual day of atonement (Yom Kippur). Without windows or lampstands, this golden room was dark, but for the glowing coals in his golden censor. God's Spirit rested above the mercy seat (the atonement cover of the ark) – and so it was, just the two of them, detached from all the people. There the man burnt incense, until the sanctuary was filled with smoke, before sprinkling the blood of the sin offerings to make atonement for Israel's sin. The Father looked on with loving, merciful patience, waiting for His Son Jesus and that memorable Passover Friday when His perfect blood became the all-time sacrifice for sin.

'There, above the cover between the two cherubim that are over the ark of the Testimony, I will meet with you and give you all my commands for the Israelites.'
Exod. 25:22

The curtain parts

It was the time of the evening sacrifice – three o'clock in the afternoon. As the paschal lamb was slain on the altar, Jesus breathed His last on the cross: 'It is finished' (John 19:30). A snag appeared in the top of the curtain and, without further warning, as if pulled by invisible hands, it tore straight down the middle (Mark 15:37–38). For the first time in many years, the mysteries of the innermost room beckoned men, women and children to walk through the gaping hole.

Jesus grants access to God's presence by a new and living way through the curtain that is His body (Heb. 10:19–29). The fullness of the Godhead dwelling in Jesus was veiled from view by His flesh, but in death His body was torn apart, to reveal His heavenly Father: 'Surely he was the Son of God!' (Matt. 27:54). And now Jesus woos us into that solitary, secret place to touch the heart of our Father.

Jesus set us a good example by frequently taking Himself off to be alone with His Father, and there are numerous other examples of how God met powerfully with people, often when they were alone (Jacob: Gen. 32:24; Moses: Exod. 3:1–5; Peter: Acts 10:9; John: Rev. 1:9). But refusing to enter the door of the secret place of prayer

'But Jesus often withdrew to lonely places and prayed ... he went up on a mountainside by himself to pray. When evening came, he was there alone ... Very early in the morning, while it was still dark, Jesus got up, left the house and went off to a solitary place, where he prayed ... Jesus ... withdrew again to a mountain by himself.'
Luke 5:16; Matt 14:23; Mark 1:35; John 6:15

is like turning our back on the blessings God has for us and for those to whom He sends us. All kinds of expectations, obligations, responsibilities and personal desires will constantly shout for our time; but the still, quiet voice of God will continue to call until we take ourselves 'beyond the curtain' and stop with Him awhile.

Upstairs prayers

There's a familiar expression of 'sending up a quick one' – a short, often urgent request fired heavenwards in the midst of a busy day. These are what I call 'upstairs prayers' but perhaps I'd better explain.

If my husband is upstairs, I shout to him up the stairwell when I'd like him to answer a question or bring me something down. He listens, and where possible shouts back his reply or throws me the requested article, but this is certainly no way to conduct a relationship! The only way I can get to know him, share intimately, receive and show love, is by making a point of being in the same place with him, shutting the door on the outside world or getting away from people. Only then can we be alone together, sitting or walking, talking or listening and enjoying each other's company; uninterrupted, unreserved and unashamed

'... when you pray, go into your room, close the door and pray to your Father, who is unseen.'
Matt. 6:6

God's heart beats in the secret, most holy place of our lives. It throbs with love desiring intimate communion. Daily He waits, but how often do we enter? Have we a tendency to pray on the run, 'shouting up the stairs' whenever we need help but without ever spending time alone with Him? Perhaps we're eager to meet other expectations or pursue worldly fulfilment, but no other relationship or activity can quench the thirst of a parched soul or nourish the hungry spirit. Spending time with God in prayer will satisfy and fulfil us beyond our wildest expectations – for that is what we are, God's holy house of prayer.

To be His house of prayer

As our awareness heightens in 'being' the temple, which by definition means that we are a house of prayer (Isa. 56:7), prayer subsequently becomes an expression of what we 'are', and not a mere chore that we feel obliged to 'do' for ten minutes or half an hour a day, week or month.

Personal prayer opens the divine channel of communication in our own lives, out of which we may then pray more effectively for others. The more we are able to share with God and hear His voice, the closer our hearts will bond with His. From this point of intimacy our prayers become energised and attuned by His all-seeing eyes, all-knowing thoughts and ever-compassionate heart.

Furthermore, God draws us into the heart of His sanctuary to empower us for the tasks in the courts. While we may long to be transformed into His likeness and be equipped for our tasks, it's the living with Him, thinking of Him, talking to Him and listening to Him that allows the Holy Spirit greater impact in and through our lives. People will see Jesus in us as we spend quality time alone in His presence, uninfluenced by externals – and that is surely our ultimate aim no matter how we may serve them.

As a house of prayer, the communication with God we enjoy in the inmost place continues to flow through the day. Prayer takes many forms, whether personal or corporate communication with God, a constant awareness of God's direction through the day's activities, the unspoken love 'prayed' over a person through eye contact or physical touch, and sometimes being the answer to prayer by helping someone practically. But we can only give out to the extent that we've already received. If we're running on empty, the power in our engine will ultimately stall. So let's spend time in His glorious presence and allow Him to feed our soul, for 'He who dwells in the shelter of the Most High will rest in the shadow of the Almighty' (Psa. 91:1).

'Blessed is the man who listens to me, watching daily at my doors, waiting at my doorway.'
Prov. 8:34

Selah

Where are you now – kneeling at God's feet, leaning up against Him, embraced in His powerful arms …? Or are you pacing the Most Holy Place, chatting mindlessly about what you've got to do but not listening very much, fiddling with the furnishings and thinking about your work, your family, your plans for the evening – barely glancing across the room to the One who is waiting patiently; desperately yearning that you'll go and sit beside Him.

'Be still, and know that I am God …' (Psa. 46:10). He yearns for your focused attention, so linger in His presence awhile. How else can you effectively meet the demands of daily responsibilities without first restoring your parched, famished and weary soul?

Here I am, Lord, come into my secret place of prayer. Forgive my fidgeting – still my soul before Your glorious presence. Speak to me, Lord, for I am listening … Amen.

15 PUTTING IT INTO PRACTICE

'One thing I ask of the LORD, this is what I seek: that I may dwell in the house of the LORD all the days of my life, to gaze upon the beauty of the LORD and to seek him in his temple.' (Psa. 27:4)

The Tale of the Temple

- Although prayer, sacrifice, worship and ministry in the temple continued throughout the day, there were set times – at the morning and evening sacrifice, Sabbaths, feasts and festivals – when everyone's attention was called to focus on worship and prayer (2 Chron. 2:4).
- 'One day Peter and John were going up to the temple at the time of prayer – at three in the afternoon' (Acts 3:1).

Temple for Today

'Will I meet the deadline? ... Mum, where are my shoes? ... Can I afford the rent? ... I need to prepare the Sunday-school talk ... Dad, will you play football with me? ... You're late, where have you been? ... Help! I'm desperate. Can I come over and talk? ... How can I get that promotion? ... What are we going to have for dinner today? ... I really ought to visit poor old Mrs Bloggs ... Have you ironed my shirt? ... What will people think of me if I don't ...?'

'The spirit is willing, but the body is weak' (Matt. 26:41)

It's one thing to believe in the importance of ministering to the Lord in the sanctuary and spending time with Him in the Most Holy Place, but putting theory into practice isn't always so easy. The list of demands on our hearts, minds and schedules is endless.

Racing from one commitment to another, how can we ever find time to 'be still', let alone, 'know that He is God' (Psa. 46:10)?

Jesus understands this struggle with time management – the pressures of juggling family, friends, work and ministry, let alone a much-needed rest! As His popularity increased, the pressure intensified from dawn until dusk with constant demands to preach, teach and heal the sick. And yet, as we saw in the previous chapter, '... Jesus often withdrew to lonely places and prayed' (Luke 5:16).

'Very early in the morning, while it was still dark, Jesus got up, left the house and went off to a solitary place, where he prayed. Simon and his companions went to look for him, and when they found him, they exclaimed: "Everyone is looking for you!" Jesus replied, "Let us go somewhere else – to the nearby villages – so that I can preach there also. That is why I have come."'
Mark 1:35–38

To leave a house may be practically or physically impossible for many. To get up early may be irrelevant for those already working night shift or at the beck and call of babies, young children or elderly dependants. But to seek a solitary place to pray is the foundation upon which the whole of Jesus' life and ministry were built. What's more, as a result of those times in close communion with His Father, He was empowered to say 'no' to anything that wasn't a part of God's plan for His life without feeling condemned or needing to justify Himself to others.

So what can we learn from the temple service to help us engage with being God's house of prayer?

The time and call for prayer

'... it is time to seek the LORD ...'
Hosea 10:12

Worshippers came to the temple throughout the day but there were set times when priests focused everyone's attention on prayer; for example, at the morning and evening sacrifice. A bellows-operated pipe organ called the *magrephah* is believed to have been struck by one of the priests on duty for preparing the Holy Place (though some think it was merely a vessel, thrown upon the floor[8]). As he did so, its distinctive tones resounded throughout the temple courts – perhaps even beyond its walls – its signal interrupting all other activity in calling the people to prayer.

Through Jesus, of course, we have the freedom to pray at any time of day or night, but I for one know that unless I discipline my diary and desires, I find myself living and praying 'on the run' instead of enjoying that quiet space. My spirit yearns for the peace of His holy sanctuary but my flesh is easily distracted to the needs of myself and others in the outer court. Nevertheless, nothing can surpass that quiet time with Jesus to develop an intimacy and depth of relationship.

So if we want to get to know Him as Scripture encourages us to and desire to be transformed into His likeness, we need the discipline of stopping still, shut away from the crowd without distraction to commune with the Lord.

'How lovely is your dwelling-place, O LORD Almighty! My soul yearns, even faints, for the courts of the LORD; my heart and my flesh cry out for the living God.'
Psa. 84:1–2

What is your *magrephah*?

So, what might be our *magrephah*, our unique call to prayer within the sanctuary? We're all very different but our Creator knows best what will grab our attention and supersede noisy distractions of tired and hectic lives. It may be an alarm clock, a set period of the day, the front door closing as children leave for school, the daily walk with the dog and so on. In asking Him what it might be, it's helpful to know whether it sounds at the same or different times, whether we recognise its tone and persistence and whether it overrides the volume of daily activity.

And as we establish and respond to our *magrephah*, we develop the fundamental purpose of our innermost being, to be a house of prayer.

The place of prayer

As the officiating priest and his assistants disappeared inside the sanctuary, everyone else knew where they should be. Whether standing on the steps leading up to the porch, positioned at one of the gates, up on the gallery or restricted to one of the courts, each person knew their familiar place of prayer. Nor was this principle restricted to the temple. In towns and villages lacking a synagogue, worshippers gathered together in a particular place that became known as their place of prayer (often by a river for ritual purification).

'On the Sabbath we went outside the city gate to the river, where we expected to find a place of prayer.'
Acts 16:13

So where is that place in God's living temple that subdues activity to focus on the Lord? As our *magrephah* sounds, where do we go? Perhaps it's the lounge, the kitchen, the bedroom, the study, a certain chair or a particular window? Or maybe it's being outside on the beach, in the woods, in the park or beside the riverbank? Is our place of prayer quiet when we want to come to it? Is it suitably warm and comfortable without sending us off to sleep? Can we ignore the telephone and doorbell? If it's somewhere outside, where can we go when it rains?

Wherever it is, God will always be waiting. And the more that we use our habitual place of prayer, the more our hearts will naturally open like flowers greeting the sunshine, flowing with praise and adoration as its familiarity compels us to pray.

Better is one day, one hour, one minute ...

'Better is one day in your courts than a thousand elsewhere ...' (Psa. 84:10). But in our life of 'years', how often do we spend a 'day' with God in the sanctuary – undisturbed and without distraction, lost in praise and joyful wonder of all that He is and does? And even if we had a free day, would we actually want to share it with God, or would we prefer to go shopping, watch a film or spend time with someone else? What or who, therefore, is really our first love?

If a day seems too long, what about an hour – just one in the 24 that we all have equally each and every day; one in the 168 or 8,736 we have each week or year? Or even a minute – one whole minute in an hour of 60, to love Him, worship Him and abandon ourselves in praise.

The more you love someone the more you want to be with him or her. The more time we give to our relationship with God, the deeper our love will grow. Start by choosing a minute, and before long you'll want a day!

Selah

Take yourself into a quiet corner of the temple. Settle yourself down and consider the following practical implications of developing your ministry in the sanctuary:

- Do you have some time each day to be alone with God – to minister to Him in the Holy Place with fragrant worship and meet Him in the secret place of prayer? If not, what changes could be made to create some space? Now commit yourself to it, just as He has committed Himself to you.

- Do you have very young children at home or elderly dependants that make this nigh on impossible? If so, do you have a Christian friend who might kindly look after them, perhaps for an hour a week, just to give you some quiet space with Jesus? If so, keep that time for Him! God understands our practical and physical limitations and will meet with us given even the slightest opportunity – but He also recognises apathy and excuses!

- If you're not there already, enter the sanctuary, close the door of your heart to outside distraction and enter the windowless world of the Most Holy Place. Dedicate afresh that special time and place where you'll meet with the Lord in private.

Lord, teach me daily to hear and to heed Your call upon my busy life, to just spend time with You, Amen.

16 LIGHT AND LIFE

'He made ten gold lampstands according to the specifications for them and placed them in the temple, five on the south side and five on the north. He made ten tables and placed them in the temple, five on the south side and five on the north.' (2 Chron. 4:7–8)

The Tale of the Temple

- The tabernacle that we mentioned in Chapter 1 had just one lampstand and one table in the Holy Place, but Solomon's Temple had ten of each.
- The solid gold lampstands (candlesticks or menorah) weighed at least 30kg, being made from one central base and shaft with six parallel branches extending three from each side. Each branch and lamp was decorated with buds and blossoms of almond flowers (Exod. 25:31–37).
- Pure, clear or white olive oil was used to fill the lamps so that the light burnt as brightly as possible (Exod. 27:20).
- The golden tables were used for the bread of the Presence (also known as shewbread, showbread or consecrated bread) and various golden utensils (Num. 4:7). They were made of acacia wood, about 0.9m long, 0.5m wide and 0.7m high, overlaid in pure gold and fitted with two gold mouldings (Exod. 25:23–25).

Temple for Today

The high priest in the temple had no choice but to withdraw from the Most Holy Place the same way that he'd entered – out through the Holy Place and back down the steps into the Court of the Priests. But nowadays it may sometimes feel like we're racing on, out of a side exit or scrambling through a window! Think about it for a moment; what's the first thing you do when you emerge from your secret place of prayer, the Most Holy Place of your heart? Do you make breakfast, flick on the TV, dash into the shower, tidy the house, check your diary, grab your briefcase, race for the train, prepare dinner or tackle an endless 'to do' list?

Whatever it is that may lure us outside, let's learn from the priests and first retrace our steps back through the Holy Place. Here we will notice some furnishings that I purposefully overlooked in our earlier approach which are useful to take us back outside – the golden lampstand and the golden table of consecrated bread; helpful symbols to keep us on track as we continue with our day.

Light from the lampstand

There's some speculation as to whether the lampstands were kept burning continually through the darkness of night or through both the day and the night. Either way, however, their light was essential to enable the priests to perform their ministries in the Holy Place. The wicks were trimmed or replaced as necessary at least twice a day and the purest olive oil used to replenish any empty lamps. And just as lamplight guided the priests serving God in the holy sanctuary so they in turn went back to the courts to guide others in His ways.

'The lamps on the pure gold lampstand before the LORD must be tended continually.'
Lev. 24:4

But Jesus arrived in those courts one day, saying, 'I am the light of the world. Whoever follows me will never walk in darkness, but will have the light of life' (John 8:12). Jesus is the lamp that lights up our lives to help guide others in His ways. We therefore need to maintain His radiance, and this we do as we follow Him.

But the Greek translation of 'follow' does not imply just believing, lagging behind a pace or two or running on ahead. Rather, it states that we remain in the same way as Him, as part of a close-knit

'For God, who said, "Let light shine out of darkness," made his light shine in our hearts to give us the light of the knowledge of the glory of God in the face of Christ.'
2 Cor. 4:6

union. Jesus wants to accompany us through a close bond of communion, and by doing so we take His light 'outside' with us. His light wasn't destined to be hidden away within our private sanctuary of prayer but to be made available to other people too. Imagine being so soaked in prayerful ministry before the Lord that our face tangibly radiated the light of His presence as we moved out into the 'courts' of our lives!

Bread of God's Presence

'Put the bread of the Presence on this table to be before me at all times.'
Exod. 25:30

The consecrated bread of the Presence, or showbread, was made from finest flour (sifted 11 times[9]) and baked as 12 flat loaves representing the 12 tribes of Israel. Every Sabbath, the fresh loaves were placed in two piles on the golden table along with incense and the golden articles used for drink offerings – a continual reminder to Israel of their complete dependence on God.

Bread is symbolic of life for it nourishes the physical body. But the consecrated bread that remained continually before God's presence symbolised both physical and spiritual life that only He could sustain. 'Then Jesus declared, "I am the bread of life. He who comes to me will never go hungry, and he who believes in me will never be thirsty" ' (John 6:35). Believing in Jesus provides hope for the future but spending time with Him now guarantees daily sustenance for our souls. And it's only as we nourish ourselves in God's presence that we have something meaningful to offer other people.

Before we leave …

So let's take a few moments to look upon these furnishings as we emerge from our secret place of prayer, daily reminders to stay dependent upon Jesus – nothing and no one else can sustain us for life in the courts as He does. Are we going to keep in step with the Lord on our way out, leaning upon Him to resource us for whatever the day may hold, or will we turn our backs on His power and love and dash right out of the door?

'But we have this treasure in jars of clay to show that this all-surpassing power is from God and not from us.'
2 Cor. 4:7

Jesus, the light of the world, inhabits God's people – humility opens the windows of the soul to let Him shine. Jesus, the bread of life, feeds God's children – absolute trust and dependence unlocks the power of heaven to do His work. Can we be so Christ-dependent that people will only see, hear and experience Jesus in His living, breathing, walking, talking, laughing, crying temple? It is certainly a goal worth pursuing, but will only develop as we remain utterly dependent upon Him in our activities throughout the day, for 'If anyone serves, he should do it with the strength God provides, so that in all things God may be praised through Jesus Christ' (1 Pet. 4:11).

Selah

Look about you before taking leave of the Holy Place. You have a choice – will you let the light of Jesus shine out of your life or veil it from view beneath a cloak of your own capability? Will you rely solely on His resources or put them to one side in pursuit of independency?

You cannot manufacture the light and life of Jesus – whatever you reveal and offer to the world will either be that which accompanies you from the Holy Place or something else of your own making. What then will it be?

Lord Jesus, You light up my darkness and nourish my soul as nothing and no one else could do. Forgive me when I foolishly seek inspiration and sustenance from bogus sources.

As I leave this secret place of prayer, thank You that Your light and life go with me into the world. Remind me to keep in step with You – neither running ahead nor lagging far behind. Help me to do this because without You, I have nothing else of significance to offer anyone I meet through the day, Amen.

17 PRAYERS OUTSIDE THE PORCH

'May your eyes be open towards this temple night and day, this place of which you said, "My Name shall be there," so that you will hear the prayer your servant prays towards this place. Hear the supplication of your servant and of your people Israel when they pray towards this place.' (1 Kings 8:29–30)

The Tale of the Temple

- Solomon built a porch along the width of the sanctuary whose entrance was flanked by two enormous bronze pillars, Jakin and Boaz. Each was topped with a lily-shaped bronze capital, festooned by a network of interwoven chains and 400 bronze pomegranates (2 Chron. 3:15–17; 4:13).
- Twelve steps led down from the front of the porch, into the Court of the Priests.[10]

Temple for Today

'Let the priests, who minister before the LORD, weep between the temple porch and the altar.'
Joel 2:17

As we emerge from the lamp-lit sanctuary, the sun is climbing the eastern sky and flooding the temple precincts with its bright, warming rays. At peace with God, attuned to His voice and dependent on His power and His love, the Spirit may now lead us in effective prayer for others.

The kings' pillar

'He erected the pillars at the portico of the temple. The pillar to the south he named Jakin and the one to the north Boaz.'
1 Kings 7:21

Having withdrawn from the Holy Place the three priests on duty took their positions outside the porch, passing Jakin and Boaz at each side of its grand entrance. Although the meaning and purpose of these magnificent bronze pillars is open to speculation it was customary for kings to stand next to one of them at important national events.

Take, for example, the young King Joash (2 Kings 11:14), or King Josiah who renewed God's covenant while standing 'by his pillar' (2 Chron. 34:8–13,31–32). Consecrating the temple and rededicating himself to the covenant, Josiah commanded the people to pledge themselves to God. This, in turn, had far-reaching effects after the damaging influence of godless kings preceding his reign.

The imagery reminds me of Paul's appeal to Timothy,

> I urge, then, first of all, that requests, prayers, intercession and thanksgiving be made for everyone – for kings and all those in authority, that we may live peaceful and quiet lives in all godliness and holiness. This is good, and pleases God our Saviour ... (1 Tim. 2:1–3)

And so as we emerge from the sanctuary these pillars remind us, 'first of all', to make intercession for kings, queens, prime ministers, presidents, church leaders 'and all those in authority'. As we pray, we can picture them standing next to a pillar, dedicating their lives to God then encouraging their people to do likewise. It happened many times in the Old Testament and it can happen again today – after all, our leaders may have changed, but God certainly hasn't, 'who wants all men to be saved and to come to a knowledge of the truth' (1 Tim. 2:4).

The priestly blessing

Returning to our ministering priests standing atop the steps outside the sanctuary, we find them with their hands raised pronouncing the priestly blessing; 'The LORD bless you and keep you; the LORD make his face shine upon you and be gracious to you; the LORD turn his face towards you and give you peace' (Num. 6:24–26). They pronounced this benediction over pilgrims in the courts, beyond the walls and over all Israel, trusting for God's promised blessing (v.27).

Indeed, it is God's desire to bless, not to harm, so in faith we can appeal for His goodness, help and mercy to fall upon those in our prayers, for 'If you, then, though you are evil, know how to give good gifts to your children, how much more will your Father in heaven give good gifts to those who ask him!' (Matt. 7:11). As we seek God's guidance in praying for other people there'll be infinite ways of doing so, but sometimes it may be helpful to begin with this priestly prayer. The depth and breadth of God's rich blessing is so broad and incomprehensible a term, we can lose the significance of its powerful potential as it trips happily off the tongue. So let's engage our thoughts and hearts in prayer for the person we have in mind, adapting the words of this scripture to seek God's blessing for their moment in hand – and even for our enemies!

'... bless those who curse you, pray for those who ill-treat you.'
Luke 6:28

Psalm of the day

After the blessing and further offerings, the Levitical choir – standing opposite but facing the priests who were still outside the sanctuary – sang the psalm of the day; on completion of which, the people bowed in worship.[11] These psalms declare God's justice, power and might, they remind us of His awesome activities and encourage us to bear fruit of righteousness (24; 48; 81; 82; 92; 93; 94). But in our living temple we're not limited to reading or singing His Word to the people; we can pray it on their behalf.

For what greater weapon have we been given in prayer than the powerful Word of God, which is '... living and active. Sharper than any double-edged sword ...' (Heb. 4:12)? It is translated as the *logos* Word (John 1) – the complete revelation of God; and also as the *rhema* Word (Luke 3:2–3) – the Holy Spirit-inspired Word of God. And so as we seek the Lord's guidance in praying for others, the Holy Spirit may choose a scripture to claim or declare on their behalf; a specific aspect of God's revealed character which empowers His inspired Word for their current situation. We can't pick verses just because they appear appropriate but we can rest on the promise that God's inspired Word will never return to Him without bearing fruit: From ' "Let there be light," and there was light' (Gen. 1:3) to sending His Word of healing (Psa. 107:20), God's Word will never return to Him without accomplishing His purposes (Isa. 55:11).

Indeed, the reading of the daily psalm inspired people to worship, so we too can hope that the ones for whom we pray by using God's Word will be brought to their knees in adoration – trusting and acknowledging God's authority, no matter the circumstances they have to face.

Further intercessions

At particular moments when the priests blessed the people and sang the daily psalm, sacrifices and offerings were presented on the altar – and perhaps we feel like that too. Perhaps we have to sacrifice time and emotion to pray for other people, especially when they're outside our immediate circle of loved ones. But it's an obligation we cannot bypass in being God's house of prayer.

Intercessions extend beyond the walls of our personal 'courts' to our country, the world at large, our persecuted Christian family and so on. But do we weep with compassion for the unsaved or are we too blinkered with our own concerns? Do we cry out to God for those in chains for the gospel, or are we blinded by our current security? Are we faithful in prayer for our missionaries abroad or more interested in personal comforts? We cannot pray for everything and everyone, but we can and must pray as the Holy Spirit leads.

'As for me, far be it from me that I should sin against the LORD by failing to pray for you …'
1 Sam. 12:23

But before we leave the arena of prayer let's pause to reflect on our liberty. For the fixed pattern, time and modes of prayer were controlled by temple law whereas Jesus provides complete freedom to pray and praise as He leads. If, for example, we haven't got time to stand at the porch first thing in the morning, we can always return to it later in the day.

But we can still learn from the principles without tying ourselves up in the chains of rigid rules, for they are written down to help and to guide, to inspire and support; to encourage our spirit to soar on wings of prayer. So let's stand on the steps, look out with God's eyes and fulfil our reason for being as His holy house of prayer.

'Now that faith has come, we are no longer under the supervision of the law … pray in the Spirit on all occasions with all kinds of prayers and requests.'
Gal. 3:25; Eph. 6:18

Selah

Come with me now to the entrance of the porch. Ask the Spirit to burden your heart with the name or names of some leaders and, as He does so, picture them standing there right next to one of those marvellous pillars. In faith, pray for their salvation, their relationship with God and the influence they have on many people.

Now turn with me and look out over the courts of your life and the arena of the world. For whom is God burdening you in prayer? He may lead you immediately in knowing how to pray, He might give you His inspired revealed Word for their situation or you may find it helpful to begin with the priestly blessing. Pause before you pray, and let Him guide your heart, will, mind and emotions.

Come back tomorrow and do likewise. Sometimes He will highlight the same people, but sometimes there will be others.

Thank You, Lord, for the tremendous gift and power of prayer. Forgive me when I do not use it to its full potential, but Holy Spirit, please teach me how, Amen.

18 SET APART

'At that time the L*ORD* *set apart the tribe of Levi to carry the ark of the covenant of the* L*ORD*, *to stand before the* L*ORD* *to minister and to pronounce blessings in his name, as they still do today.' (Deut. 10:8)*

The Tale of the Temple

- Of all the 12 tribes of Israel descending from Abraham's great-grandsons, God set apart the tribe of Levi to be His chosen servants, from which He chose Aaron and his sons to minister before Him as priests (Num. 3:12; Exod. 28:1).
- The court surrounding the sanctuary was reserved for their use, itself enclosed by a wall four courses thick; three of stone and one of cedar (2 Chron. 4:9; 1 Kings 6:36).

Temple for Today

Before we continue our temple reflections, come with me for a moment to the foot of Mount Sinai, *circa* 1445 BC (as recorded in Exod. 32).

The camp was in uproar. Indulging in ungodly revelry, shouting and screeching at a grotesque golden calf, barely anyone noticed Moses' return from atop the cloud-covered mountain. But hurling into the fire the obscene figure with its fixed lifeless stare, Moses called aloud with the voice of authority, 'Whoever is for the Lord, come to me.'

Wailing in frenzied emotion and indignant opposition, many ignored their leader's command – except one tribe who immediately stepped forward; loyal compatriots expressing their remorse. 'This is what the LORD, the God of Israel, says: "Each man strap a sword to his side. Go back and forth through the camp from one end to the other, each killing his brother and friend and neighbour" ' (v.27).

Before the sun had set in a blood-red sky, bodies littered the camp; fathers, mothers, daughters, sons, siblings, neighbours, friends – about 3,000 purged from their tents by the blade of Levitical swords. Moses addressed the faithful few, 'You have been set apart to the LORD today, for you were against your own sons and brothers, and he has blessed you this day' (v.29).

Set apart for God

The Levites chose God above everything else, not only the golden idol but even their own people, so God set them apart for a sacred ministry clearly defined through their lifestyle, dress and service in the temple.

'He made the courtyard of the priests ...'
2 Chron. 4:9

The priests alone used the innermost courtyard surrounding the sanctuary which, in addition to the altar of burnt offering and the bronze sea, housed chambers and rooms around its perimeter both for storage and temporary residence. Other Israelite men were permitted entry only as far as the Court of Israel, a narrow strip within this inner court, running parallel to the eastern wall (marked off from the Court of the Priests by a low fence and a few rising steps).

But just because a man's Levitical heritage gave him the rights to the priesthood, permission to serve was granted only provided he met certain requirements: being 'Levitically clean', reverent for God's holiness and without physical defect, for example. Nor was it a lifelong guarantee, for the sons of high priest Eli began their priestly service but were condemned for their godless behaviour (1 Sam. 2:22; 3:14; 4:16–17). So while our birthright as God's adopted children grants automatic access into the priesthood of believers, it's by no means a licence to live as we please. We're no longer citizens of this world but of heaven, and therefore have a responsibility to live accordingly, in a manner worthy of God's call – lives set apart to reveal and bring honour to our Lord.

'As a prisoner for the Lord, then, I urge you to live a life worthy of the calling you have received.'
Eph. 4:1

Distinctive devotion

If we could meet the priests as they withdrew from the Holy Place, we'd be able to smell the unique fragrance of incense permeating their clothing and hair. And if we could say hello to the priests at the altar of burnt offering, we might well rename their toiletries, 'eau de smoky aroma'! So as we live a life as God's holy temple we're going to stand out in an unholy world, distinctive through the aroma of sacrifice and the fragrance of heartfelt prayer.

> But thanks be to God, who … through us spreads everywhere the fragrance of the knowledge of him. For we are to God the aroma of Christ among those who are being saved and those who are perishing. To the one we are the smell of death; to the other, the fragrance of life. (2 Cor. 2:14–16)

For we are '… a royal priesthood … a people belonging to God … aliens and strangers in the world' (1 Pet. 2:9,11). And let's not forget that aliens and strangers simply never blend in! Daily, therefore, we must choose to be 'set apart' so that worship and service become one; distinctive in the world by our devotion in God's presence.

Ambassadors for Christ

In fact, God wants us to be distinguishable because we are His personal representatives on earth – ambassadors for Christ to the unsaved. Our aim, therefore, is to make Him known through our daily service and interaction with other people.

'We are therefore Christ's ambassadors, as though God were making his appeal through us.'
2 Cor. 5:20

Ambassadors live in a foreign country to represent the people and culture of their home. If a British ambassador kept missing appointments with foreign officials, never prepared his speeches and reports on time, was seen out every night getting drunk or picking fights and didn't stand up for the policies of the British Prime Minister, we'd sack him for his misrepresentation! But what about us – are we good ambassadors for Christ or does our compromising behaviour let Him down?

'Whatever happens, conduct yourselves in a manner worthy of the gospel of Christ.'
Phil. 1:27

To be an ambassador of Christ is to be ever mindful that our citizenship is in heaven. This world is not our true home but we live here temporarily in a tent of a body in order to make Him known.

So let's be aware as we move away from the sanctuary that it's easy to drop our guard as we go about our day. No matter how small and insignificant our activities may seem, however, they all play a part in honouring God's temple and the manifestation of Christ from within.

It's not easy to be set apart – in fact it's far simpler to find camouflage in the crowd and bow down to peer pressure – but as priests we're called to be consecrated, clothed and anointed for service, accountable to God for the way we live our lives (Lev. 21–22; 2 Cor. 5:10). God won't sack or condemn us when we make mistakes, but the nudge of His Spirit on our conscience reminds us to respect all the ways of the One we represent.

Selah

Picture yourself moving about the inner Court of the Priests. Some of your family, friends and acquaintances have entered the Court of Israel and are watching everything you do in the shadow of God's presence. How does that make you feel – eager to explain to them whom it is that you serve, excited that you've got an opportunity to welcome them to join you; or do you feel embarrassed by their looks of surprise, teasing comments or outright mirth?

Consider those people now in the light of your actual life:

- Do they even know that you're a Christian?

- Do you think they find your behaviour appealing – do they ask you lots of questions about, or express admiration for your faith, for example?

- Do you think that any teasing you endure arises because they can see through a hypocritical veneer, or simply because Christ within you makes them feel quietly uncomfortable?

You have been set apart to serve God in whichever way He chooses. Your responsibility is to keep living that life even when you stand out from the crowd, but others' resultant choice of response remains their responsibility.

Forgive me, Lord, for the times I let you down – through an undisciplined lifestyle or a preference to 'blend in'. Strengthen me in my inner being to be as confident in Your presence with others as I am when we're just alone, Amen.

19 CLOTHING THE PRIESTHOOD

'Then they brought ... to Moses [for the tabernacle] ... the woven garments worn for ministering in the sanctuary, both the sacred garments for Aaron the priest and the garments for his sons when serving as priests' (Exod 39:33,41)

The Tale of the Temple

- The high priest had special robes for his unique service: a fine linen tunic and embroidered sash; a seamless blue robe hemmed with gold bells and embroidered pomegranates; a fine linen ephod skilfully embroidered with gold, blue, purple and scarlet yarn; braided chains of pure gold to fasten the breastpiece displaying a ruby, a topaz, a beryl, a turquoise, a sapphire, an emerald, a jacinth, an agate, an amethyst, a chrysolite, an onyx and a jasper, mounted in gold filigree settings and engraved with the names of the tribes; two further onyx stones on the shoulders; a linen turban; a golden plate, tied above the forehead with blue cord, engraved, 'HOLY TO THE LORD' plus undergarments (Exod. 28:1–39,43).
- The priests also had special garments though made to a simpler pattern. They were tunics, sashes, headbands and undergarments (Exod. 28:40–43).
- They were not provided with any sandals for their feet, however, as they ministered in the temple barefoot.

Temple for Today

Clothing is more than a means to keep us warm and cover up our nudity. In fact the garments that we choose to wear can set us apart visibly from other people; they may depict a certain image or provide us with protection. And so, in the temple, the priests were given a holy dress code in which they served God. On arriving for their weekly shift, they made their way to a chamber by the Nicanor Gate, and there exchanged their travel-weary garments for their sacred priestly vestments.[12] Ready and dressed for service they then clocked on for duty.

A holy dress code

Consequently, any pilgrim entering the temple could spot a Levite instantly – set apart visibly in their sacred robes no matter the size of the milling throng. Their priestly attire was made to complement God's glory and beauty, and in so doing brought dignity and honour to their ministry and service – not because of what they had done but because of whom they worshipped. As for ministering barefoot, it merely highlighted the ethos of their sacred collection – a symbol of respect and reverence as they served in close proximity to God's almighty presence.

'Make tunics, sashes and headbands for Aaron's sons, to give them dignity and honour.'
Exod. 28:40

I'm certainly not suggesting we discard our jeans, shirts, jackets and skirts for tunic, sash and headband, nor even necessarily for clerical collar or convent habit, but I refer to the words of Paul who says:

> ... clothe yourselves with the Lord Jesus Christ ... clothe yourselves with compassion, kindness, humility, gentleness and patience ... Forgive as the Lord forgave you. And over all these virtues put on love, which binds them all together in perfect unity. (Rom. 13:14; Col. 3:12,14)

These are the clothes which bring dignity to our faith and honour to the One we worship, but is this what people actually see when they observe or interact with us? Do the attitudes with which we adorn ourselves complement the beauty of God's character or have we tarnished Christ's robes with selfishness and pride? What airs and graces, masks and mannerisms do we wear throughout our day? Do they inspire or irritate, attract or repel, welcome or warn off those that we mix with?

As servants of God and priests in His living temple, we walk 'barefoot' on holy ground every minute of our day – constantly, therefore, the attitudes that we wear should complement and revere the ways of the One who lives within.

Putting on the new

'You were taught, with regard to your former way of life, to put off your old self … and to put on the new self, created to be like God in true righteousness and holiness.'
Eph. 4:22,24

We cannot wear Christ's robes of righteousness without His help for He is our righteousness (2 Cor. 5:21) and only His Holy Spirit can clothe us accordingly, just as a young child needs help to get dressed. But as we are instructed to 'clothe ourselves' with His sacred garments it does reiterate an active decision to take off the old self and 'put on' or reveal the new.

Sometimes, our sinful nature may find these godly garments a little uncomfortable when we're faced with busy schedules, difficult problems and emotional hurts or when we're simply struggling with tiredness – times when it's tempting to change into the rags of an unsympathetic, unkind, proud, brash, impatient brand! But it's only as we choose to keep wearing Christ's attire in preference to our own that His Spirit can continue adjusting them – making them fit more snugly over our current 'shape' as we allow our tailor to nick, tuck, stitch and weave His clothing into place.

'Be dressed ready for service and keep your lamps burning …'
Luke 12:35

Rightly or wrongly, people will make judgments about us simply from first appearances so it's imperative we wear God's garments that display His nature and character – not just in Sunday services or entertaining the vicar, but through every minute of every day, whatever we do and whoever we're with.

For strength and protection

Before leaving this subject, however, let's also consider the role priests performed on the battlefield, sounding the war cry against enemy oppressors (2 Chron. 13:12). As priests of the new covenant we also engage in a battle but in addition to raising a war cry we've a responsibility to fight: 'For our struggle is not against flesh and blood, but against the rulers, against the authorities, against the powers of this dark world and against the spiritual forces of evil in the heavenly realms' (Eph. 6:12).

Would we expect our policemen to counter a violent riot without the protection of helmets, shields and clubs? Would we expect our soldiers to enter a war-zone without bullet-proof vests and weaponry? Of course not! And neither should we expect to enter our daily battle without any armour covering our sacred priestly robes: the belt of truth – secure in God's truth; the breastplate of righteousness – Christ's righteousness; the shoes of peace – walking and living out the gospel of peace; the shield of faith – protected by God's power enabling us in defence and attack; the helmet of salvation – guarding our thoughts against the enemy's lies; and the sword of the Spirit – the double-edged Word of God in prayer (Eph. 6:14–18). If we nonchalantly enter the battlefield unarmed we're offering a walking target so it's no wonder we often get shot down! But dressed and armed for service, we're ready to start our day.

'... the priests, are to blow the trumpets ... When you go into battle in your own land against an enemy who is oppressing you, sound a blast on the trumpets. Then you will be remembered by the LORD your God and rescued from your enemies.'
Num. 10:8–9

Nowadays, wearing the right name on training shoes and T-shirts, the season's latest trends and even the 'in' colour, may sneak up just a little too high on our priority list in an effort to make ourselves look 'beautiful'. But what the world perceives as outward beauty is a far and fickle cry from God's inward ideal:

> Your beauty should not come from outward adornment, such as braided hair and the wearing of gold jewellery and fine clothes. Instead, it should be that of your inner self, the unfading beauty of a gentle and quiet spirit, which is of great worth in God's sight. (1 Pet. 3:3–4)

Furthermore, fashion designers pay a small fortune in sponsoring famous stars and sports personalities to encourage them to wear their labelled products. But Jesus paid a far greater price in the hope that we'd wear His attire – an image that will never fade or go out of date; an appearance that reflects God's beauty as we minister in His house.

Selah

With the sanctuary behind you and the Nicanor Gate facing you, picture the chambers enclosed in the adjacent wall. While you cannot actually open the one containing the priestly vestments, you could place a discreet notice on your wardrobe door – a reminder each morning to pause, and ask Jesus to clothe you in compassion, kindness, humility, gentleness, patience, forgiveness and love.

Which garments do you find trickier to put on than others and which are you most likely to want to rip off first? Talk to the Lord about it.

In fact the One who designed each living temple also created a lifetime's priestly attire – garments of salvation and robes of righteousness to reflect the image of God (Psa. 132:9,16). Are you saved? – then wear your salvation with pride. Are you clothed in His robes of righteousness? – then let them stand out for everyone to see.

Now in faith, place over these garments the protective armour of God.

Forgive me, Lord, when like a little child I resist when You try to dress me; wriggling and fidgeting, throwing my arms in all directions. Here I am, Lord, standing still and ready for my temple attire, Amen.

20 PRIESTLY SERVICE

'In keeping with the ordinance of his father David, he appointed the divisions of the priests for their duties and the Levites to lead the praise and to assist the priests according to each day's requirement.' (2 Chron. 8:14)

The Tale of the Temple

- The descendants of Aaron were set apart from the tribe of Levi to serve as priests (Exod. 32:29; 40:13–15).
- The remaining Levites were also set apart for God's service, assisting the priests and overseeing more menial tasks (Num. 3; 1 Chron. 23:28–32).
- Nevertheless, whenever the number of priests was insufficient for the work, consecrated Levites could step in and minister as priests (2 Chron. 29:34).
- The many and varied tasks were divided according to which family line they belonged to within the tribe of Levi (1 Chron. 23–26).

Temple for Today

Set apart from the people by their fragrance, behaviour and dress, the priests went about their duties; but consecrating the holy things, offering sacrifices and burning incense before the Lord were just a part of their varied ministry. They prayed for the people, pronounced blessings, read and taught the Law; they trimmed the wicks and refilled the oil lamps, cleaned the sanctuary and took care of the courts and side rooms. They prepared unleavened wafers, flour, wine, oil and grain for the offerings; they dewormed wood for the altar, looked after the priestly robes and ministered as singers, musicians, gatekeepers, guards, officers, judges and treasurers. They administered lots and seals, witnessed Nazarite vows, and oversaw the work of physicians, embroiderers and maintenance men.[13]

'He appointed the priests to their duties and encouraged them in the service of the LORD's temple.'
2 Chron. 35:2

'This was their appointed order of ministering when they entered the temple of the LORD, according to the regulations prescribed for them by their forefather Aaron, as the LORD, the God of Israel, had commanded him.'
1 Chron. 24:19

And these numerous tasks weren't haphazardly distributed depending on who felt like doing them. Designated roles and responsibilities were set up for each Levite family according to God's command. They didn't try and do someone else's job or tread on each other's toes in the process – they knew their calling and quietly and reverently got on with it. Furthermore, their genealogy, age, intellect and even their physical appearance all played a part in what they could and couldn't be allowed to perform.[14]

As 'we are God's workmanship, created in Christ Jesus to do good works, which God prepared in advance for us to do' (Eph. 2:10), we need to discover and accept His chosen tasks, then simply get on and do them.

God's purposes or mine?

'... it is God who works in you to will and to act according to his good purpose.'
Phil. 2:13

So what are God's purposes for your life and mine, and are we actually pursuing them? Or are we serving our own motives and ego, trying to tailor God's will to suit our personal preference? Two of Aaron's sons began doing things their own way and it was the death of them (Lev. 10)! Rather, like the passionate priest Phinehas (Num. 25) we must work for the Lord's glory in everything we do, no matter how small and insignificant the responsibility may seem.

I believe that when God created us He put the desire in our hearts to do His will. Sometimes, however, our craving to achieve by worldly standards, other people's expectations or personal aspirations, clouds it out of view. When this happens we end up working for something or someone else – for more money, a better reputation, a positive identity, to prove our self-worth, to realise personal dreams and so on. But distractions such as these will inevitably hinder the outworking of God's purpose through our lives. If we give the enemy an inch, he'll take us a hundred miles away from the path of God's plan and we'll inevitably end up disillusioned, lacking fulfilment or warring with stress, which goes against everything that God longs to give to us – a fulfilled life (John 10:10), a light, easy yoke (Matt. 11:30) and the innermost desires of our heart (Psa. 20:4). How important it is, therefore, to make ourselves aware of, then actively engage with God's chosen tasks.

Service with a smile!

From deworming wood to burning incense, each and every task in temple ministry was special, valued and honourable to God. There was no distinction between sacred and secular because every task served to worship the Holy One dwelling at its centre. Likewise, today, every dedicated act of service is esteemed equally in God's sight, from cleaning the church to preaching the Word, from raising children to leading a government.

So, are we honestly content with what God's asked of us or do we covet the role of someone else – to be a spouse, a parent, a pastor or musician; to lead, to support, to cook or care? Imagine walking through the temple precincts and overhearing priests complaining of the heat, disgruntled mutterings from Levites cleaning the sanctuary, or grumbling resentment behind stacks of worm-ridden wood! But I wonder what God hears behind the closed doors of His living temple – 'It's not fair … I'd much rather … why is it always me, me, me? …'?

'Do everything without complaining or arguing …' says Paul to the Philippians (Phil. 2:14). In reality, however, we may find it's quite difficult to do 'everything' without even the slightest whinge because some things clash with our selfish intentions. But as our relationship with God grows stronger we develop a respect for Him and an awareness of our unique purpose which diminishes any complaining with humble, heartfelt praise.

The high priest oversaw the temple and priesthood just as our High Priest, Jesus, desires to be master over our time and efforts; it's His prerogative to assign us tasks as He sees fit, according to His design plan for each unique living temple. As God reveals His purpose, we simply need to dovetail into His will, offering our hands, feet, minds and hearts to minister within His house of prayer.

The priestly tasks were performed in order to worship God, make Him known to the people, mediate between them and honour His holiness – they did not pursue what they wanted to do but only what fulfilled God's purpose.

So what is our response when God says, 'Go', when God says, 'Do' and when God says, 'Speak'? Is our initial reaction that we

'Then I heard the voice of the Lord saying, "Whom shall I send? And who will go for us?" And I said, "Here am I. Send me!" '
Isa. 6:8

haven't got time, that we've more important things to do first or that we simply don't feel that we're capable (Exod. 4:10; Jer. 1:6; Matt. 8:21; 25:25)? Jesus said, '... I have come down from heaven not to do my will but to do the will of him who sent me ...' (John 6:38) – and that, therefore, must be our priority too.

Selah

Let's take the stairwell up through the Nicanor Gate and out on top of the wall. From this viewpoint we can look down both left and right onto the sanctuary in the Court of the Priests, the Court of the Women, the Great Outer Court and out into the skies that span the city and land beyond. Observe all the activity that goes on in and around your life every day.

Now take a pen and notepad and write down all those tasks and responsibilities that you currently do in the precincts of God's living temple, and then pray about them. You may have noticed that there's a particular job left undone – is that because you're busy trying to do someone else's?

Now jot down the things you would love to do but simply feel unable to – and why. Talk to the Lord about these things. Perhaps they're seeds of His dreams for your life, perhaps not – but don't dismiss them or covet them without first praying them through.

Here I am, Lord – use me, Amen.

21 THE COURT OF THE WOMEN

'He made ... the large court and the doors for the court, and overlaid the doors with bronze.' (2 Chron. 4:9)

The Tale of the Temple

- Solomon's Temple included two courtyards: the inner court for the priests, and a larger outer court for 'clean' Israelite worshippers.
- In the last temple, built by Herod, this court was more commonly known as the Court of the Women or the Treasury.
- Entry was gained by way of the Nicanor Gate from the Court of Israel or through the Beautiful Gate from the Great Outer Court.

Temple for Today

Moving on through the Nicanor Gate in the eastern wall, we find ourselves stepping out onto 15 semicircular marble steps that take us down to the Court of the Women.

Indeed women, provided they were 'clean', could enter this court with the men, but except for their need to approach the priest or donate monetary offerings, they were relegated to a gallery. This sat on top of a simple colonnade running around the perimeter and from the north, east and south sides they could look down and watch what was happening.[15] There was much to observe.

In addition to the infamous treasury, this court housed chambers built into each of the corners. There was one for Nazarites to make preparations before fulfilling their vows, one for healed lepers to wash before presenting themselves to the priests, one to store oil and wine for the drink offerings, and one to sort and store the wood intended for the altar of burnt offering. But just imagine at feasts and festivals how crowded this court would have been, as

'... go, show yourself to the priest and offer the sacrifices that Moses commanded for your cleansing, as a testimony to them.'
Luke 5:14

thousands of pilgrims worshipped God through such a variety of means. Picture the Levites standing on these steps at the annual Feast of Tabernacles, leading the people with praise and worship in singing the Psalms of Ascent (120–134); expressions of trust and joyful anticipation of meeting God in His temple. With great gusto the amassed Israelites celebrated God's faithfulness, giving thanks for the recent harvest and praying for future rains. Indeed, this court was frequently filled with praise and thanksgiving as pilgrims joined together, raising their hearts and voices to extol their mighty God.

24/7 worship

'Worship the LORD with gladness; come before him with joyful songs ... Enter his gates with thanksgiving and his courts with praise; give thanks to him and praise his name.'
Psa. 100:2,4

Thus the temple continually reinforced its ethos of worship which weaved its reverent way throughout the holy precincts – from the intimacy of the sanctuary to the bustle of the Outer Court, worship remained a vital principle.

And yet despite their aroused expectation in prayer and praise, when the One they anticipated arrived in their midst, they simply could not recognise Him. With their faces turned to the sanctuary, they rejoiced with anticipation for the day of God's salvation when His Spirit would pour out on His people (Isa. 12:3; Joel 2:28). But many could not continue to praise when, faced with God's answer, they did not recognise Him, standing right alongside them.

To what degree, therefore, do we still limit focused worship to personal devotions or corporate gatherings in church? Perhaps, as we've come out of the sanctuary we've built up our faith with prayer and praise but now as we stand among people and responsibilities, we fail to recognise His ongoing presence in the courts of our life – and as a result our sense of worship diminishes with the day.

The demands of our 'outer court' loom ever closer on the other side of the wall, which could so easily take our focus off maintaining communion with God, but remaining in an attitude of worship elevates our hearts, minds, words and deeds to His higher power and purpose as we continue to praise the One who dwells within. Worship energises and focuses our spirits on whom it is that we serve – even as we walk out to face an endless conveyor belt of dirty dishes, a 'Mount Everest' of ironing, the thirtieth year in the same office or the countless times we've performed some skill or duty. So '... whatever you do, whether in word or deed, do it all in the name of the Lord Jesus, giving thanks to God the Father through him ... work at it with all your heart, as working for the Lord, not for men ...' (Col. 3:17,23).

The Women's Gallery

In the eyes of God, all men and women, old and young are esteemed equal. And yet I wonder if sometimes we build ourselves a 'gallery' – preferring the role of a distant observer rather than getting engrossed in a life of abandoned praise. Or maybe we go there because we feel inadequate; unworthy of living up to the Christian life of passionate, fervent worship.

If you feel this applies to you then what might be your 'gallery'? What stops you from joining in with others and fulfilling the purpose God calls you to in the courts of His living temple? I am by nature an extremely shy person, which often sends me running up those steps when God is calling me into an unknown crowd. But it can also be fear of failure, inability to trust God's promises, a sense of rejection, a lack of self-worth, insufficient confidence to get on with the work assigned to us, shame or embarrassment by the way that we look physically or even what we wear. We feel safe in God's presence when it's just the two of us but struggle to keep trusting and praising Him as we walk out into the day.

'Not until halfway through the Feast did Jesus go up to the temple courts and begin to teach'.
John 7:14

So if you're sitting in that gallery reading this book, may I invite you to stand up and lean over the parapet; to look down from your viewpoint into the court below. Can you see Him? Jesus has come to the temple and He's looking up at the gallery. He's waving, in fact He's beckoning you down to join Him, calling out; 'If anyone is thirsty, let him come to me and drink. Whoever believes in me, as the Scripture has said, streams of living water will flow from within him' (John 7:37–38). This is His promise to you – that you will overflow with the power of His Spirit throughout your day. But first you have to walk down the steps and go to Him and 'drink'.

'I will sacrifice a thank-offering to you and call on the name of the Lord. I will fulfil my vows to the Lord in the presence of all his people, in the courts of the house of the Lord – in your midst, O Jerusalem. Praise the Lord.'
Psa. 116:17–19

Do you recognise God's coming to you, or is previous experience and personal expectation blinding you to His presence? Drink afresh of His Spirit regularly during the day, renew the power and vitality of His living temple, and quench the developing thirst of your soul.

The psalmist encourages us to '... seek his face always' (Psa. 105:4); not just in the sanctuary of personal devotion, not just singing songs on Sunday, but always – every waking hour of every God-given day. 'From the rising of the sun to the place where it sets, the name of the LORD is to be praised' (Psa. 113:3). Call out to Him in faith, a defiant cry against desolate feelings. Bring songs and shouts of jubilation to declare His wonderful name, for a sacrifice of praise brings peace beyond our wildest imagination. For, even if we've not built a 'gallery', this court has something to say – to continually remain in that ethos of worship each hour of every day.

Selah

Welcome to the Court of the Women! Walk with me down the 15 marble steps into its precincts of adoring praise. 'Blessed are those you choose and bring near to live in your courts! We are filled with the good things of your house, of your holy temple' (Psa. 65:4).

But listen, there's someone knocking – or should I say battering – at the Beautiful Gate right in front of you. And whoever it is demands you attend to the tasks that await your day.

Before you open the gate, though, take a look just beside you; leaning against a pillar, Jesus is lovingly watching you. No matter where you move in this court, to the treasury, chambers, steps or colonnade, He always seems to be there – waiting, watching and wearing His gentle, compassionate smile. He can see that you're in a dilemma with the stress of a busy schedule commanding you onwards while the peace of intimate prayer tries to pull you back inside.

Jesus moves towards you now and reaches out His hand. Will you take it and walk out with Him into your day or abandon Him here in your compartment of prayer and praise?

Put your hand in His, and whatever crops up you can simply turn your head and see His glorious face right next to you – an inspiring picture that puts the stress and strain right back into perspective.

Lord, I realise how quickly I 'lose' that sense of reverent prayer and worship once I leave the sanctuary for my daily responsibilities. Please remind me to keep close to and focused on Your constant presence throughout every day. Jesus, You worshipped our Father in and through everything that You did and said. Please teach and show me how to do the same, Amen.

22 TEMPLE TREASURIES

'He gave him the plans of all that the Spirit had put in his mind ... for the treasuries of the temple of God and for the treasuries for the dedicated things.' (1 Chron. 28:12)

The Tale of the Temple

- The temple treasuries were included in God's specified plan for His temple. They were built into Solomon's larger court and Herod's Court of the Women.
- In Herod's Temple they consisted of 13 trumpet-shaped, brass collection boxes fixed along its western wall. Each one was allocated for a specific monetary offering – nine obligatory and four voluntary.[16]
- These offerings included the temple tax that originated from the half-shekel contribution paid by Israelites of 20 years of age and older, whenever a census was taken (Exod. 30:11–16), but which evolved to become the annual mandatory donation towards temple ministry.
- By Jesus' lifetime it was valued at two drachmas and exchanged by temple money-changers from pilgrims visiting Jerusalem at Passover who hadn't already paid it to the tax collectors where they lived (Matt. 17:24–25).

Temple for Today

There's one more consideration to be made in this Court of the Women before we move on, and that is the subject of money. Perhaps that comes as a surprise in a book devoted to inward sacrifice and prayer, but money is also a means of worship because giving back to God plays a significant part in honouring His name.

In fact, the temple certainly wasn't short of a shekel or two! In addition to the wealth of reserves collected and dedicated to the Lord's house from years of successful battle booty, pilgrims brought practical gifts which could be used in temple ministry or sold to provide a monetary donation. They also brought money to buy their animal sacrifices, contributions to the ongoing necessities of ministry and additional freewill voluntary gifts, particularly on major feast days. And as if that wasn't enough, they were all obliged to pay the annual temple tax or tribute.

Administering God's treasuries

One of the Levitical responsibilities was therefore administering the temple treasuries. Pilgrims brought their tithes to God and the priests kept it safe in the depository chests, awaiting its ongoing employment.

'Their fellow Levites were in charge of the treasuries of the house of God and the treasuries for the dedicated things.'
1 Chron. 26:20

We cannot send a cheque or monthly standing order addressed to a heavenly bank account for God's personal use, but within our lives are various treasury chests – purses, wallets, bank accounts, savings and various types of capital in which God keeps His financial resources. As stewards of His earthly treasury, He trusts us to invest it wisely, in accordance with His instructions.

As our Father, He takes responsibility to provide for what we need to live, that which nourishes, protects, educates and maintains His living temple – our homes, clothing, food and so on. But many of us, particularly in the West, are also blessed with a great deal more than our daily needs require, and why else but to resource God's work and workers? The greater our financial resources, therefore, the greater our responsibility of stewardship.

So, as priests of God's living temple, are we that scrupulous with the money placed with us or more inclined towards filling our personal pockets? The people gave 'freely and wholeheartedly' (1 Chron. 29:9), but dare I say that our giving to God's work might sometimes be described as 'minimal and begrudging'? And yet the Levites did not deviate from the task of collecting and administering the temple treasuries, and nor should we (2 Chron. 8:15).

Good stewardship

When Jesus sat down in the Court of the Women, He watched and knew how much rich and poor were placing into the treasuries – and He's still watching today; both the amount we put in and the amount we hold back! He commended a poor widow who gave everything she had as her devoted expression of worship, and she remains a wonderful example for all of us today (Mark 12:41–44). So with that in mind, let's take a brief look at our role as His temple stewards.

' "Bring the whole tithe into the storehouse, that there may be food in my house. Test me in this," says the LORD Almighty, "and see if I will not throw open the floodgates of heaven and pour out so much blessing that you will not have room enough for it." '
Mal. 3:10

First, we can give only according to the amount entrusted to us. We cannot give more than we have but neither should we give less than we're able to – each one should give 'according to their ability' (Ezra 2:69).

Second, we must trust the Holy Spirit to guide us where and in whom He wants to invest the financial resources deposited with us, over and above that which we need for daily necessities and the loving gifts our Father gives us for personal enjoyment. Irresponsible stewards use their money to line their own pockets or bury it where it's of no use to anyone (Ezek. 22:12,25,27–29). Good stewards invest wisely according to and on behalf of their Master's instructions.

Third, we ought to understand that we'll find the release to give freely, wholeheartedly and with great rejoicing only as we learn to trust increasingly in God's loving faithfulness. '... a defender of widows, is God in his holy dwelling' (Psa. 68:5) – the widow had no fear for her future as she placed in the treasury her very last coin as she believed He would care for all of her needs. God hasn't changed – so He'll always take care of ours too.

> 'All these things have I given willingly and with honest intent. And now I have seen with joy how willingly your people who are here

> have given to you' ... Then David said to the whole assembly, 'Praise the LORD your God.' So they all praised the LORD, the God of their fathers; they bowed low and fell prostrate before the LORD and the king. (1 Chron. 29:17,20)

Generous, joyful giving to God is well documented throughout Scripture especially in relation to the temple, for it is yet another means of worship – of bowing down, prostrating all we have in reverence of the One we call Lord. Both the message and the practical expression of His love require funding to resource and support its work and workers. And so God assigns differing amounts to each one of us, entrusting us to pass it on and not hoard it for ourselves.

We cannot take one iota of our material possessions to our future heavenly home – but we can take the results of how well we've used them, storing up our treasure in heaven (Matt. 6:19–20). It merely leaves us to ask, therefore, how much has God entrusted to our treasuries and how well are we administering them.

'Naked I came from my mother's womb, and naked I shall depart.'
Job 1:21

Selah

Walk with me beneath the colonnade towards the shiny, trumpet-shaped treasury chests. Stop in front of one and answer me this question: How much income do you receive each year – income from a salary, whether yours or that of your spouse, income from investments, pensions, gifts and any other source of financial revenue?

Perhaps, to your relief, you can't answer that to my face, or perhaps your immediate response is 'That is none of your business'! But God doesn't need to ask that question because He gave it to you in the first place. All He needs to know is, 'How much are you going to give back?'

You are His living temple incorporating His treasury. He won't necessarily expect or ask you to give away every last penny but He does look beyond any outward façade, observing the intentions of your heart.

As a unique house of prayer, God will reveal how He wants to use your resources. Are you willing, therefore, to surrender everything back to His lordship, or do you still hold on to those additional savings to pay for 'your' future, a perceived security or all those current comforts? God is completely trustworthy, the most secure investment you could ever make!

Lord, I long to excel in serving You with the talents You've given to me but teach me also to excel in the grace of giving, that Your Name and Your work may be effective in and through the treasuries entrusted to my care, Amen. (Based on 2 Cor. 8:7)

23 THE GREAT OUTER COURT

'... Jesus was in the temple area walking in Solomon's Colonnade.' (John 10:23)

The Tale of the Temple

- After the Maccabean revolt (167 BC), the temple was rededicated and its perimeter extended.[17]
- Herod expanded it yet further, constructing a vast outer court (which we now call the Court of the Gentiles or the Great Outer Court), almost doubling the temple plateau. Roofed cloisters ran right the way round the inside wall consisting of double rows of marble pillars, each 11.5m high.[18]
- Solomon's Colonnade ran along the eastern wall while the impressive Royal Stoa (or Royal Porch) ran along the southern wall. This magnificent structure incorporated four rows of 40 columns, each 30.5m high, and housed the Jewish ruling council (or Sanhedrin) within its sealed-off eastern corner (John 11:47; Acts 4:15–18).[19]
- Traders selling birds and animals for use in sacrifice and exchanging temple currency were permitted to set up their stalls in this vast outer court.

Temple for Today

Having walked through the length of the Court of the Women, we can now pass through the Beautiful Gate and into the Great Outer Court.

It was here in this court that Jesus:

> ... found men selling cattle, sheep and doves, and others sitting at tables exchanging money. So he made a whip out of cords, and drove all from the temple area, both sheep and cattle; he scattered the coins of the money changers and overturned their tables. To those who sold doves he said, 'Get these out of here! How dare you turn my Father's house into a market! ... 'It is written,' he said to them, ' "My house will be a house of prayer"; but you have made it "a den of robbers" ' (John 2:14–16; Luke 19:46).

Den of thieves?

'... I have heard your prayer and have chosen this place for myself as a temple for sacrifices ... my house will be called a house of prayer ...'
2 Chron. 7:12; Isa. 56:7

The temple housed all manner of activities long before Jesus stepped into its precincts, but it was never called a house of teaching or a house of singing; or of markets, priests, purifications, tithes, festivals and so on. These activities were intrinsic to temple ministry and service but they were simply intended to focus the attention on its core function, the *raison d'être* of God's house – to be a temple for sacrifices and a house of prayer.

With this purpose in mind, therefore, what would we expect to find within this vast enclosure – hushed reverent worshippers, perhaps? In reality, the bustle of visitors, particularly during the feasts, was phenomenal. Take, for example, the Passover celebrations during New Testament times when as many as 2.5 to 3 million pilgrims made their way to Jerusalem![20] Furthermore, there were the calls of market-traders amidst flapping doves, bleating lambs, lowing cattle and jangling coins. But while their merchandise was necessary for sacrifice, the ethos of worship was obscured by profit-making activities in pursuit of selfish gain. And that's why Jesus got angry!

Similarly, the outer court of our lives incorporates the bustle of daily activity, jobs and responsibilities intrinsic to our unique ministry. Nevertheless, whatever we do and say in our outer court should all point towards and magnify the One who dwells within.

Zeal for God's house ...

No one was permitted to offer sacrifices in this court, and relatively few people spent time there to pray, but that was no excuse for irreverent or ill-motivated behaviour.

'His disciples remembered that it is written: "Zeal for your house will consume me." '
John 2:17

Shouting to a friend across the expanse of a library, playing a stereo full-blast in a hospital ward or making compost in the kitchen will not actually demolish the library, hospital or house. They will, however, play havoc with the ethos of reading, healing or homemaking with inappropriate, utterly distracting noise, behaviour and odour. Jesus didn't blitz the market because it sat in Herod's extravagant extension but rather because the essence of certain activities totally disregarded the innate temple function. So instead of being drawn into the heart of worship, pilgrims' attention was too easily distracted by the noise and expense of mal-motivated traders.

Jesus remains as zealous for His Father's house as He was in AD 30 but perhaps the mere thought of asking Him to overturn any unseemly tables in our lives may be somewhat disconcerting. Rest assured, however, that He does it with great love and care in His passion to help us sanctify His Father's living temple.

House for all nations

And let's not forget that the temple was built as a house of prayer 'for all nations' (Isa. 56:7); where foreigners who committed themselves to God could worship alongside His people. No doubt there were many such folk for its magnificent splendour and God's supreme reputation soon spread far and wide (1 Kings 10:1). Gentile believers, who were moved in spirit to visit Mount Moriah, were permitted access to Herod's Outer Court, provided they revered and acknowledged the ways of the One who dwelt at its centre.

'Now there were some Greeks among those who went up to worship at the Feast. They came to Philip, who was from Bethsaida in Galilee, with a request. "Sir," they said, "we would like to see Jesus." '
John 12:20–21

Moreover, it was this renowned Jerusalem Temple that introduced the world to Jesus – the perfect living temple of God's Holy Spirit; Someone who pulled far greater crowds than the 1960s

'Beatle-mania'. Admittedly His fame spread quickly owing to His miraculous powers, but His love, compassion, grace and humility were magnetic; attracting rich and poor, Pharisee and farmer, leader and leper, to want to find out more.

So too, our lives – our temple ministries – have potential to draw others to worship. But unless we build in submission to the Spirit we may find that we're putting 'all nations' off, so robbing them of God's promised joy. Let's therefore take time in our vast outer court to 'become all things to all men so that by all possible means [we] might save some' (1 Cor. 9:22); prepared to go to any length to inspire and encourage those who seek God in His sanctuary.

And so, as we consider the fact that we're God's house of prayer, we begin to understand that prayer is far more than mere words – it's the deep communion in song, in silence, in service and in rest that pervades each hour of our day. Whether we're dancing with praise, flat on our face in awe, caring for our family, serving in our church or workplace, we can fulfil God's purposes in being His house of prayer.

Perhaps we've let things slip in the outer courts, and 'traders' are distracting our attention, robbing the very nature of God's house. But, like the godly King Hezekiah, let's restore and consecrate every area of our lives; for 'In everything that he undertook in the service of God's temple and in obedience to the law and the commands, he sought his God and worked wholeheartedly. And so he prospered' (2 Chron. 31:21) – and so can we!

Selah

Pause awhile, to sit among these grand porches and colonnades. Look around about you at what goes on in this court. How would you feel if Jesus came and walked through the colonnades of your life? Would there be any hint of embarrassment, guilt or shame?

Be completely honest with yourself and with God, and consider whether you've any habits or characteristics that discourage you, your Christian friends or non-believers from drawing closer to God.

Lord, please come and walk through the gateways, cloisters and expanse of my life. I realise that every part of me needs to point to the holy sanctuary and focus the attention onto You. Turn over the tables in my life that I may restore an appropriate spirit of prayer and sacrifice no matter where I am or who I am with, Amen.

24 THE 'WORD' FOR THE COURTS

'Not until halfway through the Feast did Jesus go up to the temple courts and begin to teach. The Jews were amazed and asked, "How did this man get such learning without having studied?" ' (John 7:14–15)

The Tale of the Temple

- In addition to the priests reading, teaching and administering the Law from positions nearer the sanctuary, rabbis and pilgrims enjoyed ongoing debate of God's Law within the shady cloisters; particularly those of the Outer Court and especially Solomon's Colonnade.
- At the age of 12, Jesus found a place among them where He listened, learned and talked with exceptional understanding for one so young (Luke 2:41–47).
- As an adult, Jesus often taught here as He mingled with priests, teachers, Pharisees and pilgrims (Matt. 21:23–46; Luke 20:1; John 7:14).
- The apostles also spent time in the courts, sharing their message, and teaching how Old Testament prophecy had been fulfilled through Jesus, the promised Messiah (Acts 3:11–26; 5:20–21).

Temple for Today

One of the roles of the temple priests was to read and teach the commands of Scripture. Ezra, 'devoted himself to the study and observance of the Law of the LORD, and to teaching its decrees and laws in Israel' (Ezra 7:10) and as he read from it, the returning exiles responded with worship (Neh. 8:1–6). Meanwhile, certain other Levites also read from it, '... making it clear and giving the meaning so that the people could understand what was being read' (8:8). And within the shade of the magnificent cloisters surrounding the Outer Court, many a rabbi and pilgrim would read, teach or discuss the complexities of God's Law.

But one fine day, a boy on the brink of adulthood at a mere 12 years of age, visited the temple courts and sat among the teachers – listening to them carefully and asking poignant questions. Years later, He frequently returned, teaching the people in the temple courts and explaining God's Law (Luke 2:42,46–47; 20:1). Jesus – fully human, yet fully God; the Word made flesh mingling with the pilgrims, fulfilling Old Testament prophecy and igniting the New. Some perceived God's glory in the humble man standing before them while others chose to ignore and even hate it.

The Word made flesh

In the popular game of charades, somebody acts out the syllables and words of a chosen film, book title or song, while others have to guess what they're trying to say through their performance. It's a helpful image as we consider the Word made flesh – God's will and ways, His truth and love, perfectly expressed through the body and life of Jesus. For:

> In the beginning was the Word, and the Word was with God, and the Word was God ... The Word became flesh and made his dwelling among us. We have seen his glory, the glory of the One and Only, who came from the Father, full of grace and truth. (John 1:1,14)

'Let the word of Christ dwell in you richly ...'
Col. 3:16

Until we make a personal commitment, the Bible is merely a collection of 66 books-worth of historical typescript. But as Jesus, the Word, makes His dwelling in our lives, we engage with His Spirit and the written Word becomes alive, revealing God's glory through its pages; just as He revealed it to believers 2,000 years ago (John 17:5–8).

But as priests of the new covenant, how can we share the Word with others if we're not first letting it live and take effect in and through our own lives; if we're not seeking to understand its application to the culture and world in which we live today?

Berean or Thessalonian?

'Now the Bereans were of more noble character than the Thessalonians, for they received the message with great eagerness and examined the Scriptures every day to see if what Paul said was true.'
Acts 17:11

The Bereans, in contrast to the Thessalonians, were commended for their study of the Scriptures, but could that be said of you and of me? Perhaps the mere mention of 'study' sends us racing in another direction! But it need not be brain-achingly boring with God's Spirit as our teacher and some useful tools to help us:

- Bible-reading notes, for example, are a helpful resource to discipline a daily feeding on a portion of God's Word. A trip to your local Christian bookstore will hopefully offer a vast array of publications available nowadays and you may be surprised by both the quality and variety of notes available.

- For those who prefer their own reading plan, however, it's still important to study unfamiliar passages as well as all the favourites. God's Word traces the path of salvation from the beginning of time to the beginning of eternity – we could miss out on valuable teaching and inspiration if we limited our scope to just a few books that we find easier or more comforting to read than others.

'... keep my words and store up my commands within you. Keep my commands and you will live; guard my teachings as the apple of your eye. Bind them on your fingers; write them on the tablet of your heart.'
Prov. 7:1–3

- Sometimes it's helpful to read a number of chapters at once to grasp the bigger picture of a letter or story. At other times, however, it's important to chew over just a verse or two, asking the Spirit to take its truth and relevance deep into our soul.

- Memorisation is another invaluable tool – to be able to pray or quote snippets of Scripture during the day is a priceless key to building up our own faith and sharing it with others. While we may not have the remarkable memory of nineteenth-century hymn writer Fanny Crosby, who by the age of ten could apparently quote the first four books of the Old and New Testaments, we have no excuse to ignore the challenge to store up God's Word in our hearts.

- Furthermore, by reading appropriate chapters of a Bible handbook alongside Scripture we collect user-friendly helpful insights that unveil the world of the Bible to our twenty-first-century experience.[21]

The Word in our temple

So what if any thieves, therefore, rob God's temple of its spiritual nourishment (Matt. 4:4), guiding light (Psa. 119:105) and mighty sword (Heb. 4:12)? What's happening in the shade of our 'cloisters'? Are we engaging with the Word, reading and meditating upon it, asking the Spirit to breathe life into the truths that fill our minds and hearts? Or are we ignoring it, even criticising or debating its relevance and authenticity?

The Word of God is flawless and penetrates the depth of our being, preparing us for sweet communion with Jesus. It teaches the heart, comforts the soul, disciplines the flesh, guides the will and offers a sure hope for the future – so if we have a Bible, let's not waste a moment longer to spend time within its pages.

Selah

Find a quiet place to sit down and rest your back against one of the marble pillars in this great outer court, closing your eyes to the distractions of all its activity. Jesus wants to join you here, to sit down beside you and talk through the Scriptures, but what, if anything, robs you of that time – lack of inclination, lack of space in the day …?

Now open the eyes of your heart and begin to mull over His Word – can you see Jesus walking through its pages? He was there in Genesis 1 and He's waiting for you in Revelation 22. What is He showing you about Himself and His Father? How is He using it to speak into your heart? Is it comforting, disciplining, guiding or confusing?

Do you attend some kind of mid-week fellowship or home group where you can meet with others beneath these cloisters and discuss it further?

The Word – Jesus – became flesh and, in so doing, personalised the Scriptures to the people He met in the Great Outer Court. The Word can become personal to you today too as His Holy Spirit brings it alive in your heart. But if you need to put some 'flesh' on it – something tangible and memorable – why not 'personalise' your Bible?

You could underline key scriptures and/or use different coloured highlighters to emphasise certain themes, and start writing your own cross-reference notes or helpful information in the margins. Whatever you do, make it personal and meaningful to you.

Thank You, Lord, for the gift of Your Word. Forgive me for the times I've taken it for granted or been lazy in my approach. By the inspiration of Your Spirit please teach me Your ways and Your will as I determine to spend more time in its pages. And so may its truths then build themselves into the fabric of my life, Your living temple, Amen.

25 GUARD THE GATES

'The gatekeepers had been assigned to their positions of trust by David and Samuel the seer. They and their descendants were in charge of guarding the gates of the house of the LORD … Lots were cast for each gate, according to their families, young and old alike.' (1 Chron. 9:22–23; 26:13)

The Tale of the Temple

- As indicated on the 'Summarised Outline of Herod's Temple' at the beginning of this book, there were many gates leading into Herod's Great Outer Court, but the principal entrance used by pilgrims were the gigantic Holdah Gates in the southern wall.
- Depending on their state of purification, Israelites could cross the *chel* (a terrace in the Great Outer Court), and access the Court of the Women via the principal entrance on the eastern side known as the Beautiful Gate – a vast, ornate structure of Corinthian brass requiring 20 men to open and close its hefty double doors.[22]
- Suitably 'clean' men could then enter through the Nicanor Gate into the Court of Israel, but only the priests could approach and enter the sanctuary and only the high priest, just once a year, could pass beyond the veil into the Most Holy Place.

Temple for Today

During my teens I attended a girl's grammar school where, on commencing my O-level studies, some lessons were shared with boys. And so, as giggly teenagers, we relished the short walk up to their school for music.

On one occasion, I was so distracted by a fascinating conversation with my friend that I failed to notice a small doggy-deposit on the pavement. It was only once we were inside the classroom that its foul stench began filling my nostrils. Discreetly looking around at my neighbours' shoes I searched for the culprit – only to find out it was me! Horrified, I flushed scarlet, felt nauseous and watched what little street-credibility I owned vanish with the moment.

To my shame, I desperately tried to scrape off the evidence onto the side of the chair leg, pretending it was left by a previous student; but there was nothing I could do to mask that awful smell from permeating the room. At long last the lesson finished and with great embarrassment I followed the trace of my dirty footprint back outside the building!

I can laugh at the memory now but it comes back to mind as I consider the ethos of God's holy temple. It causes me to consider which parts of my life pollute a far greater building than a classroom to teach youngsters music.

The Levitical guard

'He also stationed doorkeepers at the gates of the LORD's temple so that no-one who was in any way unclean might enter.'
2 Chron. 23:19

The temple was destined to be a holy dwelling and therefore required a system of guards to keep watch over all of its gateways. From the outermost court to the innermost sanctuary they supervised pilgrims' adherence to strict rabbinical laws concerning who might enter the holy site and who would be deemed unclean – whether from giving birth, coming into contact with a dead body, having various skin diseases or discharges, mildew-contaminated fabrics and so on (Lev. 12–15; 21:11).

Singing in the choir or sprinkling incense on the golden altar sound far more exciting and esteemed assignments than guarding the gates, and yet these chosen Levites '... were capable men with the strength to do the work ...' (1 Chron. 26:8). So let's not underestimate the significance of their task, for if they failed to keep out any 'unclean' person, the whole site and ministry risked being defiled.

But as numerous as they were, temple regulations weren't infallible. Punishment for wilful disregard resulted in 40 lashes, the 'rebel's beating' (stoning to death) or being cut off from the Israelites forever. The guards too were subject to beating if their captain, with overall responsibility for supervising temple security, caught them sleeping on the job – some even had their garments set alight![23]

Once again, I breathe a sigh of relief that Christ set us free from such laws and regulations! But those serious repercussions for being caught off guard highlights an important principle that we oughtn't to take too lightly, besieged as we are by the lapsed morals and motives of mankind. So, 'Consider now, for the LORD has chosen you to build a temple as a sanctuary' (1 Chron. 28:10) – a sanctuary from the world's pollution where a Holy God may dwell.

Gateways of the soul

Before we can set a guard in place we need to pinpoint the gateways. And these we find in our living temple through sight, sound, touch, taste and smell, plus the inner spawning of thoughts and dreams. Admittedly, we can't always help seeing and hearing things in our vast outer court but how quickly do we prevent them approaching the sanctuary through the 'Beautiful Gate' of the mind – the principal feed into the heart of our temple?

'Do not conform any longer to the pattern of this world, but be transformed by the renewing of your mind.'
Rom. 12:2

We live in a world where opinions of what is right or wrong blur increasingly at the edges as declining standards are accepted as the norm. A constant watch on our gateways is therefore paramount. Looking at inappropriate television, books or magazines, listening to gossip or sordid jokes, satisfying our taste for excess food or drink, touching people improperly, sniffing addictive substances and dwelling on impure thoughts or plans for revenge are just some of the polluting habits, desires and self-satisfying patterns that bombard a life dedicated to pleasing and honouring God.

We too, therefore, can place a guard upon our gateways and Scripture teaches us how:

> Love the LORD your God with all your heart and with all your soul and with all your strength. These commandments that I give you today are to be upon your hearts ... Write them on the door-frames of your houses and on your gates. (Deut. 6:5,6,9)

Memorising and applying the rules of godly entry at our 'doorposts' inspects everything that we see, hear, touch, taste, smell and ponder upon. In fact, we've an abundance of biblical instruction for living upright, godly lives which we're each responsible to consider and put into practice. And when anything attempts to sneak past the safeguard of loving, pleasing and honouring God in His holy temple it sounds a shrill alarm that brings into play the overall 'captain' – that which supervises how well we guard against ungodly infiltration.

The captain of the guard

'... fight the good fight, holding on to faith and a good conscience. Some have rejected these and so have shipwrecked their faith.'
1 Tim. 1:18–19

'So I strive always to keep my conscience clear before God and man.'
Acts 24:16

The captain of the guard in our living temple is our God-given conscience; the voice of our spirit communing with our Father sensing what is right and wrong. My conscience gets pricked as soon as I see a police car in my rear-view mirror, even when I'm driving within the speed limit! Sadly, however, my fear of offending God doesn't always equate to my fear of a speeding ticket.

When our conscience sounds an alarm we need only confess our sins to renew it, but if we leave them festering we may find ourselves grappling with a slippery slide of compromise. Refusing to pay attention to it until the decay sets in is like delaying a dental visit when we've got bad teeth, by which time we're suffering the painful consequences! A fine-tuned conscience spots contamination a long way off but one that's ignored permits all manner of unseemly things into the holy sanctuary before we notice the subsequent damage.

So how is our conscience – our captain of the guard – being refined or restricted today? Are we feeding it with human postulations or biblical truth? If we're reading Scripture, to what extent are we putting it into practice? To actively engage and grow, the conscience demands a love for God that far outweighs temptations to compromise, but such love requires more than feelings; it's a conscious act of the will.

What do we bring into God's house, therefore, that makes Him screw up His nostrils? What do we intentionally or unwittingly bring into the sanctuary that defiles it? Are we filling our lives with treasure or with trash?

Let's clear out the temple of the dross we've welcomed in, confess our sins at the bronze sea and so renew our conscience. And '… whatever is true, whatever is noble, whatever is right, whatever is pure, whatever is lovely, whatever is admirable – if anything is excellent or praiseworthy – think about such things' (Phil 4:8).

Selah

Standing here in your outer court, take a good sniff of the air. When I was in that classroom I didn't need to actually see the excrement, I (and others) could smell it!

What causes a stench to God with the pollution you bring into His temple?

It took just a second to pick up the offence, and a few minutes to invade the classroom – how quickly do you allow pollutants to spread throughout His sanctuary?

I was distracted when I stepped in the mess, not realising what I had done. What distracts you from keeping close watch on the things that bombard God's temple?

No matter how hard you try, you cannot hide or make excuses for what you 'walk into' God's house. How quickly do you confess and what efforts do you make to repent?

Just one tiny smudge caused havoc to an entire classroom. How many people aside of the Lord are affected by the contamination?

How many unsightly footprints walk across your life and who might follow in your footsteps?

Lord, if only I would maintain that ethos of worship how much easier it would be to guard against ungodly infiltration. But 'who can discern his errors? Forgive my hidden faults. Keep your servant also from wilful sins; may they not rule over me', Amen. (Psa. 19:12–13)

26 TEMPLE UNDER ATTACK

'He carried to Babylon all the articles from the temple of God, both large and small, and the treasures of the LORD's temple ... They set fire to God's temple and broke down the wall of Jerusalem ...'
(2 Chron. 36:18–19)

The Tale of the Temple

- In *circa* 587–586 BC,[24] King Nebuchadnezzar of Babylon ransacked Solomon's Temple (2 Chron. 36:17–19).
- Its successor, rebuilt by Zerubbabel, stood for 500 years but faced its own downfall at the hands of the Roman General Pompey, in 63 BC.
- The last standing temple, built by Herod the Great, was also destroyed by the Romans, in AD 70, under the command of Emperor Titus of Rome.
- But it wasn't just Israel's enemies that disrupted temple ministry for even their own ungodly kings caused havoc and disruption, through abusing God's holy ways and by shutting the temple doors (2 Kings 16; 2 Chron. 28:24).

Temple for Today

Perhaps it seems like too much effort to keep a close watch on the gates of God's temple, but history proves what dire consequences such apathy can reap. Israel was warned time and again concerning the possible onslaught of the enemy but '... they mocked God's messengers, despised his words and scoffed at his prophets until the wrath of the LORD was aroused against his people and there was no remedy' (2 Chron. 36:16). King Nebuchadnezzar attacked and ransacked, then carried them off to Babylon. The Israelites became his servants and the temple treasures his gold.

We too may find we're in times of exile, feeling distanced from God's presence – in bondage to people or circumstances with His temple in ruins at our feet. Looking back, we remember the days of rejoicing in His Spirit, when we served with energy and enthusiasm and when others were drawn to God because of our testimony and witness. What changed though? Who or what stripped His temple of treasure and eroded His house of prayer?

What happened?

As we shall see, many things can wreak havoc with our lives, but sin was the primary cause of temple desecration – a turning away from the Lord. If, therefore, His living temple is malfunctioning owing to persistent, unrepented habits, then we'd better do something about it. After all, the history of the temple, the teaching of Scripture and even nature itself prove that we'll always reap what we sow. Have you ever sowed tomato seed then harvested lettuce? Of course not, so 'The one who sows to please his sinful nature, from that nature will reap destruction; the one who sows to please the Spirit, from the Spirit will reap eternal life' (Gal. 6:8). Those who sow to maintain God's temple will reap a holy dwelling-place; but those who sow to please themselves will reap their self-made consequences.

Not that it's always our fault, is it? Sometimes we come under 'attack' because of the sins of other people. But the effects of the immediate onslaught will be drastically reduced provided that we forgive. The sin of unforgiveness eats through the heart like woodworm as it bores painfully through our soul, but irreparable damage will transpire only if we hold on to the hurt – so let's not leave it festering.

The ravages of storms

'I have told you these things, so that in me you may have peace. In this world you will have trouble. But take heart! I have overcome the world.'
John 16:33

But other winds of adversity 'attack' the purpose of God's dwelling, aside of personal sin; robbing us of the joy of ministering in God's house. Jesus never promised us an easy life but He did say we'd experience trouble. Whether it be rejection, marriage breakdown, financial insecurity, persecution for our faith, bereavement, childlessness, singleness, job loss, long-term illness or disability and so on, we may experience days, months or even years when the bleakest winter settles upon the season of our soul.

Our response to what we find difficult will vary. Some people will let it push them to their knees in the Most Holy Place, finding within the only true source of comfort for the present and security for the future. And when they do this God strengthens His battered temple and uses it as an encouragement to help and witness to others. But some of us will react with panic, racing away from the sanctuary to find solace elsewhere. It may at the time seem the easiest option but not always the most productive.

'The Lord is a refuge for the oppressed, a stronghold in times of trouble. Those who know your name will trust in you, for you, Lord, have never forsaken those who seek you.'
Psa. 9:9–10

Satan also longs to inflict damage on our lives – but he cannot enter the gates unless we let him. He'll assail us from the outside but we have all the means necessary to counter him provided we choose to do so: faith that we are protected by Christ's blood, the maintenance of a vigilant guard, living our life in the shadow of God's love, training ourselves for the battlefield and wearing our armour with confidence.

'Be self-controlled and alert. Your enemy the devil prowls around like a roaring lion looking for someone to devour.'
1 Pet. 5:8

But sometimes the demise of temple ministry simply boils down to us. For one reason or another we've robbed the treasuries and shut the temple doors – just like King Ahaz (2 Chron. 28:24). Could this be us today? Have we intentionally or otherwise closed the doors of the holy place and extinguished the light in the lamps? Has the once-fragrant air turned musty and cold in the absence of fragrant incense?

If life has caved in around us for any of these reasons, it may be impossible to see God. Nevertheless, we believe in faith that He's right there in the middle of it with us, albeit veiled from sight by the 'fallout'. In time, the smog will settle and we'll see Him again more clearly; God Almighty, dusty and dirty as He works among the rubble to rebuild His living temple.

'... my Spirit remains among you. Do not fear.'
Hag. 2:5

As a convalescent needs time out to rejuvenate, so storm damage may also disrupt activities in our courts. But as Zerubbabel considered the challenging and daunting task of rebuilding the Jerusalem Temple, the Lord encouraged Him: 'Be strong' (Hag 2:4), 'I am with you' (v.4), 'I will grant peace' (v. 9), 'I will bless you' (v.19) and 'I have chosen you' (v.23).

God is with you too, and will strengthen you to rebuild His holy dwelling-place.

Selah

What or who broke down your guard bringing havoc to God's holy dwelling – who stole the treasures, closed the sanctuary of prayer or left the building in ruins?

Take courage to be honest with God. If it was personal sin or apathy then use this time to confess and establish how you might now change your ways. If it's other people's sin then ask the Lord to help you forgive them – even if you can't *feel* it in your heart. If it's some kind of loss then talk to the Lord about it. He's sitting here with you, even if you can't quite see or feel Him. He's weeping with you, feeling your pain but willing and waiting to take all your fear and promising great hope for your future.

There's no rush. He's got as long as you need to talk it all through.

At times like this it can be difficult and almost impossible to feel we're able to pray. So perhaps today, you'd let me join you, put my arm around your shoulder and pray on your behalf:

Here we both are, Lord, and the scene doesn't look too pretty. I see condemnation, emotional and physical hurt, a spiritual desert and the relentless ache of an empty soul. Open our eyes, Lord, to see You sitting with us – open our hearts and hands to feel Your loving touch ...

... Thank You for Your beloved child who is leaning up against me – take my place, Lord, and help them to lean on You. I know that You love and accept us just the way we are but please help your child believe that too. Pour out Your Holy Spirit on them and grant them Your perfect peace, Amen.

27 RETURN AND REBUILD

'So the LORD stirred up ... the spirit of the whole remnant of the people. They came and began work on the house of the LORD Almighty, their God ...' (Hag. 1:14)

The Tale of the Temple

- In the first year of his reign, Cyrus, king of Persia, proclaimed throughout his realm that God had appointed him to build a temple in Jerusalem and that the Israelites should be freed to return in order to complete the work (Ezra 1:1–4).
- Those whose hearts had been moved prepared to return to Jerusalem for the task of rebuilding (v.5).
- The king provided for the work by giving them silver, gold, goods, livestock, and many articles from Solomon's Temple that had been stolen by Nebuchadnezzar (vv.4,7,11)
- First they began to rebuild the altar of burnt offering (3:1–3) and then the foundation. But the people became discouraged by their enemies and stalled the work for another 16 years (3:7–4:24).[25]
- Further unsuccessful attempts were made by their enemies to stall the construction but God turned it around for the benefit of His people (5:3–6:10).
- Thus the work continued and the temple was rebuilt (6:14–15).

Temple for Today

Seventy years in exile, as Jeremiah foretold – 70 long years of waiting, hoping, trusting for the remainder of the prophecy to be fulfilled. It was a dark time in Israelite history, a bleak period of desperate yearning for God to restore His people to His holy city. Bent and bruised with age, but not broken; the fading light of youthful memory smouldering, but not snuffed out – the Israelites awaited their promised freedom. And they were not to be disappointed.

'This is what the LORD says: "When seventy years are completed for Babylon, I will come to you and fulfil my gracious promise to bring you back to this place."'
Jer. 29:10

Rebuilding the altar

'... everyone whose heart God had moved – prepared to go up and build the house of the LORD in Jerusalem' (Ezra 1:5). So has God been stirring your heart? And if so, will you respond and prepare to rebuild His house in your life?

No matter the reason we might find ourselves in exile from God's presence with His temple seemingly in ruins, He longs to bring us back to Himself and rebuild His holy dwelling-place – but we have to want to do that too. God has promised to complete the good work He began in us (Phil. 1:6) but it's a two-way responsibility; a partnership working together to build His temple for sacrifices and a holy house of prayer.

'Despite their fear of the peoples around them, they built the altar on its foundation and sacrificed burnt offerings on it to the LORD, both the morning and evening sacrifices.'
Ezra 3:3

As always, God will start with the altar of burnt offering – our choice to let Him back onto the building site. We may feel painfully vulnerable with open wounds still raw from recent attack but let's trust Him to take the fragments of our life and remake them, not into what had been before, but into something even better. And if you find this difficult, 'Consider him who endured such opposition from sinful men, so that you will not grow weary and lose heart' (Heb. 12:3).

God is with us and will help restore our lives into His holy dwelling-place. He'll provide all the resources needed for His work and restore everything necessary that the enemy has stolen.

Dealing with discouragement

Despite Haggai's encouraging prophecy, the elders who had known the former glory of Solomon's Temple wept with despair when they saw what they perceived would be its less impressive successor (Ezra 3:12). If we too are constantly looking back to how we used to be or what we used to do, we may not hear or see what God has planned for our future. As He walks us back from exile, therefore, and rebuilds His living temple, let's not simply wait for what had been in the past but expect something greater than we've ever known before.

'See, I am doing a new thing! Now it springs up; do you not perceive it? I am making a way in the desert and streams in the wasteland.'
Isa. 43:19

And be warned, for when the enemy gets wind of our revived commitment he'll be sure to come and sniff out the opposition

(Ezra 4:1–2)! Even the people who lived nearby tried to discourage Zerubbabel (Ezra 4:4–5). So perhaps we'll be ridiculed for our renewed zeal, misunderstood, pressurised to compromise and so on, but take care or the work could grind to a halt by the pressure of human fear.

God will never give up on His work, and nor should we, so let's build up our defences against such discouragements. First, we can determine to be diligent in what God is challenging us to do – focused application of His instructions avoids distraction from outside forces. Second, when Jesus was tempted to despair He asked his closest friends to draw near, to keep watch and pray (Mark 14:34) – likewise, let's rally our faithful friends; their prayerful support may well be the lift we need to overcome the next hurdle.

'The men in charge of the work were diligent, and the repairs progressed under them.'
2 Chron. 24:13

'And in this place I will grant peace'

Further unsuccessful attempts were made by Israel's enemies to hinder the building project but God turned it around for the benefit of His people (Ezra 5:3–6:10). The enemy will never give up trying to frustrate the Lord's work so our struggles may not disappear, but God will stand over us in defence of His beloved temple, turning around our unseemly circumstances for our own benefit.

God isn't blind to our personal limitations and weaknesses, the distractions other people might put in our way or the work of the evil one. He could remove them from our path in an instant if He so chose but rather prefers that we rely on His strength to bring Him honour and fulfil His purpose – ' "Not by might nor by power, but by my Spirit," says the LORD Almighty' (Zech. 4:6). Let's not keep returning to old patterns of behaviour or rely on human plans, methods and opinions, but let's rely on the Holy Spirit to guide us in rebuilding the living temple – and let's do it without hesitation.

God's temple may lie shattered at His feet but He wants to rebuild it one stone at a time. Trust Him to take the fragments of your life and reconstruct them, not into what had been before, but into something even greater, for ' "The glory of this present house will be greater than the glory of the former house … And in this place I will grant peace," declares the LORD Almighty' (Hag. 2:9).

Various ungodly kings desecrated and damaged Solomon's

Temple before its ultimate destruction, but King Hezekiah was one who restored and repaired it (2 Chron. 29–31). The subsequent effect of his actions rippled across the nation. As the doors reopened, the priests and Levites were consecrated for service, the city officials brought sacrificial offerings, and the people of Israel demolished their false altars, resurrecting the festivals ordained by the Lord.

As a result of his commitment to the temple, therefore, religious leaders, government heads and the population at large recommitted themselves to God. Surely we need look no further for encouragement today to rebuild the walls and reopen the doors of God's house of prayer!

Selah

If you're still sitting among the temple debris feeling hopeless and alone, then lift up your head and look about you. You are not alone. God is right there with you putting one stone back on another with perfect precision; replacing and securing the pillars by the strength of His mighty arm; restoring all the treasures that you thought were lost forever …

… and now He's calling you to stand up and help. To work alongside Him in all that He wants to rebuild. Are you willing to get your hands dirty in order to put things straight? Are you prepared to let go of the old so that He can take you on to the new?

> [Be] confident of this, that he who began a good work in you will carry it on to completion until the day of Christ Jesus … [so] press on towards the goal to win the prize for which God has called [you] heavenwards in Christ Jesus. (Phil. 1:6; 3:14)

Lord, I have nothing I can offer at this moment other than a seed of faith. Take it, nurture it and build it up into something new and beautiful that will give You immense pleasure, Amen.

28 GOLDEN OR GODLY GLORY?

' "The glory of this present house will be greater than the glory of the former house," says the LORD Almighty.' (Hag. 2:9)

The Tale of the Temple

- The magnificent splendour of Solomon's Temple – its grand entranceways, marble floors, gigantic pillars, gold-plated walls, gold and silver utensils, precious gemstones, fine priestly clothing and so on – earned for themselves a famous reputation among other kings, queens and countries (1 Chron. 22:5; 2 Chron. 9:1–4).
- After the completion of Zerubbabel's Temple, those who looked at its outward appearance grieved for Solomon's splendour; but those who recognised God's presence and protection rejoiced in His loving mercy (Ezra 3:10–13).
- Herod's Temple was by far the most magnificent to look at but, as we saw in Chapter 14, the Most Holy Place was empty of the ark of the covenant with its golden cherubim and the cloud of God's glorious presence.

Temple for Today

'The temple I am going to build will be great, because our God is greater than all other gods.'
2 Chron. 2:5

Walk through the temple in your mind's eye and indulge your imagination with its magnificent splendour – the white marble, burnished bronze, fine linen, exquisite embroidery, gleaming gold, shining silver and multi-coloured gemstones.

Indeed, the architecture and furnishings were unquestionably remarkable and inordinately expensive, but its intrinsic feature and priceless quality was determined by God's presence within. Its purpose was to be a temple of sacrifice and house of prayer but its construction and ministry arose from a spirit of holiness, quintessential of the Holy God whom it served.

Sadly, however, people became more enamoured with its elegance and religious rites than with the honour of the One whom it housed. Israel's devotion lapsed as priests and people hankered after their own pleasures and worshipped other idols, barely noticing when the cloud of God's glory disappeared from the Most Holy Place (Ezek. 10). But the true glory of God's last Jerusalem Temple arose from something new – from the presence of Jesus walking through its courts; for 'The Son is the radiance of God's glory and the exact representation of his being ...' (Heb. 1:3).

Misplaced glory

Jeremiah reprimanded Israel for putting their trust in the existence of God's house rather than God Himself, but is it possible we might also trust more in ourselves than in God? And if so, do we thereby gain our self-worth and identity from the temple ministry and appearance rather than His presence within? 'Do not trust in deceptive words and say, "This is the temple of the LORD, the temple of the LORD, the temple of the LORD!" ' (Jer. 7:4).

Our identity, that sense of value and self-worth, can arise from many sources. To name just a few examples, it may derive from our role as a parent or spouse, from our service at church or in the community, from pursuing a certain physique, wearing fashionable clothes, enjoying good health, earning a good salary, achieving success at work, keeping a tidy home, preaching a cracking sermon, singing beautiful solos, being needed by other people or from skills as a musician, flower-arranger, youth worker, artist, cook and so on. But our true worth arises from God's love for us, and the glory of His temple from our relationship with and submission to His Holy Spirit living within.

'As he was leaving the temple, one of his disciples said to him, "Look, Teacher! What massive stones! What magnificent buildings!"... "I tell you that one greater than the temple is here." '

Mark 13:1; Matt. 12:6

'You blind fools! Which is greater: the gold, or the temple that makes the gold sacred?'

Matt. 23:17

Contentment in the shadow of God's glory

It's easy to say we find our worth in God but it's not until it's tested that we find out where it really lies. Loss of health, work, home or a special relationship can strip us of our outward identity overnight, leaving our self-worth vulnerably naked. If, however, we seek now to establish our identity in Christ, then we need have no fear of it ever being stripped away in the future, no matter how our circumstances may change.

Of course there's nothing wrong in having an attractive appearance, being skilled, successful or popular and so on; in fact the physical care we take with our health and the effort we put into work and relationships is important in serving God to the best of our ability. But if any of these things become the security upon which we build our self-esteem, then they transfer our focus away from God's glory by shifting it onto ourselves.

'Because of your temple at Jerusalem kings will bring you gifts.'
Psa. 68:29

Living our lives as God's temple, however, and representing Him, releases us from peer pressure, a need to be complimented and the stressful striving for fickle standards put on us by the world. It frees us to be the person God wants us to be, enabling Him to make His appeal through our lives in His chosen culture and setting, and with the talents and resources He's provided. And so we need to be known by God and let God's glory be known through us.

I am Christ within me

'I have been crucified with Christ and I no longer live, but Christ lives in me.'
Gal. 2:20

To do this, Paul encourages us to '... become mature, attaining to the whole measure of the fulness of Christ' who Himself was filled to the measure of the fulness of God (Eph. 4:13; 3:19). How else can we be filled to such a measure but by dying to self so that His Spirit may have an ever-increasing capacity to fill our living temple with His glory?

I am nothing and can be of no lasting help to anyone unless Christ lives in me and works out His purposes through my life. I am Christ within me – it's only as I allow Him to reign and be Himself in and through God's temple that I then understand and find fulfilment in the purpose God planned for my life. Therein lies the 'glory' of His temple; therein lies my identity; therein lies the unshakeable truths to feed my need for self-worth.

As ambassadors of God's kingdom He needs our hands to provide His help, our face to radiate His smile, our arms to enfold His embrace, our feet to take His message to the world. No matter how we look and no matter what we do, our ultimate question needs to be: am I more concerned that people see me, or Jesus living His life through me? '... just as we have borne the likeness of the earthly man, so shall we bear the likeness of the man from heaven' (1 Cor. 15:49) – so Jesus, in me, is who I need to be!

When Solomon completed everything according to God's instructions, God filled the temple with the cloud of His glory. When we're obedient and follow His pattern and way of holiness, we too will be filled to ever-increasing measure with the fulness of His glory. So let's seek that fulness of God in and through our lives as we dedicate afresh the living temple of our living God; for '... we, who with unveiled faces all reflect the Lord's glory, are being transformed into his likeness with ever-increasing glory, which comes from the Lord, who is the Spirit' (2 Cor. 3:18).

Selah

Having walked through the temple in your mind's eye, now walk through the courts, chambers and sanctuary of your own life – God's living temple. What areas of its architecture, decor, ministry, service or relationships might be competing for the true glory residing within your heart?

If any or all of these things were removed, how would you feel about yourself – who you are, your purpose in life, your standing among your family, friends and peers? To what degree would your self-esteem be affected?

Are you trying to win the approval of people, or of God? Are you trying to please others? Paul says, 'If I were still trying to please men, I would not be a servant of Christ' (Gal. 1:10).

Lord, I confess that I rely too heavily on the opinions of other people for my sense of identity and self-worth. Please help me to be at peace with myself, just as You want and made me to be; to let You work both in and through my life so that others will see and worship You.

Lord Jesus, I receive in faith, the glory of the Holy Spirit that our Father gave to you (John 17:22), Amen.

29 DEDICATING THE TEMPLE

'When Solomon finished praying, fire came down from heaven and consumed the burnt offering and the sacrifices, and the glory of the LORD filled the temple. The priests could not enter the temple of the LORD because the glory of the LORD filled it.' (2 Chron. 7:1–2)

The Tale of the Temple

- Solomon completed the work of the temple in all its detail then furnished it and filled the treasuries with all that David had dedicated (2 Chron. 5:1).
- The ark of the covenant was brought up from the City of David and placed beneath the wings of the golden cherubim in the Most Holy Place (2 Chron. 5:1–8).
- Levites played cymbals, harps, lyres, trumpets and sang their praises to God (2 Chron. 5:12–13), including Psalm 30 which was written by David especially for the occasion.
- Solomon prayed a prayer of dedication and fire fell from heaven consuming the burnt offerings, then the cloud of God's glory filled the sanctuary (2 Chron. 6–7:2).
- Consequently, the Israelites fell to their knees with their faces to the ground, worshipping and thanking God (2 Chron. 7:3).

Temple for Today

The word 'dedicate' means: to devote (oneself, one's time etc.) wholly to a special purpose or cause; commit wholeheartedly or unreservedly.[26]

Dedication isn't such a popular word nowadays where broken marriage vows, government U-turns and needless 'sickies' from work challenge the commitment that 'dedication' originally implied. Nor should it be confused with a one-off recognition of a defined purpose – like dedicating a boat as a cruise ship, a building as a hospital or royalty to their throne. Rather it acknowledges wholehearted commitment from that moment forward.

And so Solomon prayed and offered many sacrifices as the ark of the covenant was placed into the Most Holy Place; corporately dedicating Israel to the ongoing consecration, ministry and service of God's dwelling-place on earth. The temple was built, but its purpose had only just begun – to be a temple for sacrifices and a house of prayer that God might dwell among His people and make Himself known to all nations.

'Then Solomon said, "The Lord has said that he would dwell in a dark cloud; I have built a magnificent temple for you, a place for you to dwell for ever." '
2 Chron. 6:1–2

Dedication: fully committed

Years later, when Solomon and future kings turned their hearts away from God onto wealth, power and idols, the temple lost its significance and was inevitably desecrated, ransacked and even destroyed. But those kings who renewed their commitment and dedicated temple ministry found favour in God's sight and influence among His people. Thus, the temple served its purpose in God's unfolding plan of salvation throughout many generations – and it still does today, provided we uphold our commitment to doing it His way.

When we first made our profession of faith, the purpose of God's temple in our lives had only just begun. But dedication – the ongoing commitment to a purpose – implies that our '... hearts must be fully committed to the Lord our God, to live by his decrees and obey his commands ...' (1 Kings 8:61).

'Solomon showed his love for the Lord by walking according to the statutes of his father David ...'
1 Kings 3:3

All those good incentives we've written down or spoken about in prayer must now be put into action, for 'Now that you know these things, you will be blessed if you do them' (John 13:17). We can sing songs of worship or pray prayers of commitment, but unless we're living accordingly our words are regrettably worthless. So 'Whatever the God of heaven has prescribed, let it be done with diligence for the temple of the God of heaven' (Ezra 7:23).

Indeed, everything in the temple was completed according to God's precise instructions and so He filled His house with the cloud of His glory. We can't expect to keep living life our way and still be filled to full measure with God – if He is to become greater within us then 'self' must surely become less (John 3:30).

Dedication: To making Him known

'But will God really dwell on earth with men? The heavens, even the highest heavens, cannot contain you. How much less this temple that I have built!'
2 Chron. 6:18

Even so, Solomon recognised that no building, no matter how exquisite, can ever contain almighty, omniscient God, who penetrates every part of His creation; even the highest heavens could not contain Him. God can make His presence known in all kinds of ways – through the glories of nature, pillars of cloud and fire, quiet whispers, angels and so on; and yet, as we've seen, He also chooses to reveal Himself through temples.

'Yet give attention to your servant's prayer and his plea for mercy, O LORD my God. Hear the cry and the prayer that your servant is praying in your presence' (2 Chron. 6:19). God may be omniscient but the temple was the one site in the world where people could approach Him with confidence in prayer. It didn't limit God's all-embracing power and authority but it encouraged people to draw close to Him, thereby preparing them for personal relationship with an awesomely powerful God.

'... without holiness no-one will see the Lord.'
Heb. 12:14

And that is what we are, the visible dwelling-place of God living among humankind. He who lives in a high and holy place also dwells with him or her who is contrite and lowly in spirit (Isa. 57:15). We cannot restrict Him, but we can reflect Him. God cannot be squeezed into a format of a relationship of our own making, but He loves to dwell within and manifest Himself through each of His dedicated unique temples.

Dedication: until the day we go home

'May your eyes be open towards this temple day and night, this place of which you said you would put your Name there. May you hear the prayer your servant prays towards this place.'
2 Chron. 6:20

As this book draws to a close I trust that we too shall choose to dedicate our living temple to the ongoing consecration, ministry and service of God. But genuine dedication involves wholehearted devotion long after we've put the book back on the shelf. Dedicating the temple is more than a one-off prayer that results in overnight transformation. It's a day-by-day commitment to knowing God in His sanctuary, serving Him in the courts, and making His glory known among the people with whom we live – a responsibility that cannot be taken lightly.

One day we shall step out of its courts for the very last time and enter our eternal home in heaven. Not until then will the temple be completed, not until then will we see the fulness of His glory face to face. But, let's persevere in the same way as Solomon who carried out all the work necessary, '... from the day the foundation of the temple of the LORD was laid until its completion' (2 Chron. 8:16).

Postscript:

When my daughter brought home annual school reports, the first thing we looked at was the grade for effort – as far as we were concerned, the acceptable norms of success became secondary provided she was doing the best that she could do.

We'll never achieve perfection in this world but God seeks out a willing spirit in what He knows are weak and weary bodies. So what keeps us going when the going gets tough, what picks us up when we trip over? The anticipation of that glorious day when we'll hear Him speak those words, 'Well done, good and faithful servant! ... Come and share your master's happiness!' (Matt. 25:21).

Selah

I must leave you alone now to walk once more through the precincts of your life, God's living temple. But as you do so, dedicate each area of your body, service, talents, resources, relationships, worship, testimony and witness – a commitment to the ongoing maintenance and ministry of God's temple of sacrifice and holy house of prayer.

Lord, there is no God like You – even the highest heavens cannot contain Your almighty presence. And yet, You desire to live in my heart as I kneel in faith and submission to Jesus.

Take this life, Lord – every sinew, feeling, talent and trait – dedicated to Your holy service, Amen.

Journal

'But your hearts must be fully committed to the LORD our God, to live by his decrees and obey his commands, as at this time.' (1 Kings 8:61)

PART THREE

THE TEMPLE IN HEAVEN

30 TEMPLE IN HEAVEN

'... Now the dwelling of God is with men, and he will live with them ...' (Rev. 21:3)

The Tale of the Temple

- Before the end of time, God will judge the nations from His temple in heaven (Rev. 15:5–16:1).
- After judgment, however, heaven, earth and temples, will all pass away to be replaced with a new heaven, a new earth and the new Jerusalem (Rev. 21:1–4,22).

Temple for Today

Temples come and temples go. Solomon's, Zerubbabel's, Herod's and even yours and mine, have been and will one day return earth to earth, ashes to ashes, dust to dust. We've learnt about the past and considered how it applies to the present, but where is it all leading?

God dwells in our lives by His Spirit while sitting on His throne in the temple of heaven. It's a high and lofty place of His divine presence from where He'll send His final judgment on earth. But one day, the old shall be replaced by a new heaven and earth where temples shall cease to be.

'Then I heard a loud voice from the temple saying to the seven angels, "Go, pour out the seven bowls of God's wrath on the earth." '
Rev. 16:1

'I did not see a temple in the city, because the Lord God Almighty and the Lamb are its temple' (Rev. 21:22). At long last we see the climax of God's unfolding plan of salvation bursting from Scripture's final pages. And just as Eden had no need of a temple neither will the perfection of eternity, where God will be perfectly satisfied dwelling face-to-face with humankind.

Temples in transit

'Set your minds on things above, not on earthly things. For you died, and your life is now hidden with Christ in God. When Christ, who is your life, appears, then you also will appear with him in glory.'
Col. 3:2–4

The awesome thought of our glorious future can leave one feeling light-headed, and yet isn't it easy to get bogged down with the humdrum of here and now? So throughout our lifetime of maintenance, ministry and service of God's earthly dwelling-place, let's never lose sight of the temple's temporary nature. Let's 'fix our eyes not on what is seen, but on what is unseen. For what is seen is temporary, but what is unseen is eternal' (2 Cor. 4:18).

Heaven should surely be our deepest desire, living in God's presence without clouds, curtains or bodily barriers veiling Him from view. But is it? When life goes well, preoccupation with its goodness and blessings may trick us into thinking it will last forever, so much so that we don't give a thought to our long-term future. And when life goes badly, problems may dishearten us, dragging us into earthbound depths of hopeless despair. But remember that no matter how beautiful or barren the wilderness of our journey, how smooth or stony the path that we tread, God's glory beckons us daily on the horizon. So let's lift up our eyes and feast on the promise of His perpetual presence.

'I am torn between the two: I desire to depart and be with Christ, which is better by far; but it is more necessary for you that I remain in the body.'
Phil. 1:23–24

Paul longed to be clothed with his heavenly dwelling (2 Cor. 5:2), yet one of his many aspirations was that, by life or death, Christ would be exalted in his body – God's temple (Phil. 1:20). He knew he must first complete the tasks assigned to him until the day when his longing would be fulfilled to go and live with Jesus. What about us? Are we so taken up with today that we've lost the importance of where it's all going? Or are we so desperate to leave and be with God that we're failing to fulfil His present purpose? Let's press on with the tasks of today while keeping an eye on eternity, which helps us fulfil our purpose in the present by keeping it all in perspective.

Pressing on towards that goal

'You need to persevere so that when you have done the will of God, you will receive what he has promised.'
Heb. 10:36

My daughter is currently studying at university to be a vet. Throughout her childhood she longed to be able to help sick animals and made the most of every opportunity to befriend, handle and care for anything covered with fur, feathers or hair! As I write, she's studying for her end-of-first-year exams but has another four years to go. Her room is littered with diagrams explaining the finer cellular details of the trachea and intestine, the complicated workings of the muscles in a dog's leg and reams of information on pharmaceutical drugs. She longs to be able to practise with real, live animals but the first two years behind a desk and microscope are essential to fulfilling her longer-term dream. Particular mundane studies sometimes drag her down, attacking her motivation – how tempting it is to just drop it all, meet up with friends and 'party'! But keeping one eye on the tasks before her she keeps the other on her veterinary goal – and that's what keeps her going.

We too have to choose to uphold the purpose and witness of God's holy temple in and through our daily lives, but building that altar of choice and offering our daily self-sacrifice are far from easy. So when we're distracted with pleasure-filled days, downhearted with the sorrows or fed up with the mundane, let's remember why we're here, what He wants us to do and where it's ultimately heading.

Take-off to eternity

I hope this book has inspired you to make ready a temple befitting of its holy resident, one which is filled to the measure with God. But as we fulfil our potential in doing so, let's never lose sight of that glorious hope to come.

This life and its temples can never compare to the future glory of being in His presence. Although many seek satisfaction in the temporary here and now, it's not what we were created for. We, who believe, can find full satisfaction for this life and the next as we consciously engage with God's Holy Spirit dwelling within, for 'it is God who has made us for this very purpose and has given us the Spirit as a deposit, guaranteeing what is to come' (2 Cor. 5:5).

So pause with me for *Selah* just one more time, as today we take a walk through a somewhat different temple – the life that awaits in a brand-new earth, face to face with our Father. Nothing even comes close to this outstanding hope for our future.

Selah

How can I even begin to describe what our future may be like, let alone put it into words? So forgive me, this once, for handing the task to a man who has seen it for himself – here in the words of John's Revelation let us look through the keyhole of time to the temple-less place where we shall one day be heading:

> It shone with the glory of God, and its brilliance was like that of a very precious jewel, like a jasper, clear as crystal. It had a great, high wall with twelve gates, and with twelve angels at the gates. On the gates were written the names of the twelve tribes of Israel … The wall was made of jasper, and the city of pure gold, as pure as glass. The foundations of the city walls were decorated with every kind of precious stone. The first foundation was jasper, the second sapphire, the third chalcedony, the fourth emerald, the fifth sardonyx, the sixth carnelian, the seventh chrysolite, the eighth beryl, the ninth topaz, the tenth chrysoprase, the eleventh jacinth, and the twelfth amethyst. The twelve gates were twelve pearls, each gate made of a single pearl. The great street of the city was of pure gold, like transparent glass. I did not see a temple in the city, because the Lord God Almighty and the Lamb are its temple. The city does not need the sun or the moon to shine on it, for the glory of God gives it light, and the Lamb is its lamp. The nations will walk by its light, and the kings of the earth will bring their splendour into it. On no day will its gates ever be shut, for there will be no night there. The glory and honour of the nations will be brought into it. Nothing impure will ever enter it, nor will anyone who does what is shameful or deceitful, but only those whose names are written in the Lamb's book of life … He who testifies to these things says, 'Yes, I am coming soon ...' (Rev 21:11–12,18–27; 22:20)

Return here often and take time to wander through this beautiful city. Bask in the light of God's promised brilliance to maintain your perspective on 'today' while renewing your hope for 'tomorrow'.

'... Amen. Come, Lord Jesus' (Rev. 22:20).

Journal

'I did not see a temple in the city, because the Lord God Almighty and the Lamb are its temple.' (Rev 21:22)

BIBLIOGRAPHY

All biblical references are quoted from:
The Holy Bible, New International Version (London: Hodder & Stoughton, 1986)

Alexander, David and Pat (eds), *The Lion Handbook to the Bible* (Hertfordshire: Lion Publishing, 1973; 2nd revised edn, 1983)

Alexander, Pat (ed.), *The Lion Encyclopedia of the Bible* (Hertfordshire: Lion Publishing, 1978; 2nd revised edn, 1986)

Edersheim, Alfred, *The Temple: Its Ministries and Services* (Massachusetts: Hendrickson, 1994)

Hanks, Patrick (ed.), *Collins Dictionary of the English Language* (Glasgow: William Collins, 1979)

Ilumina: digitally animated Bible and encyclopedia suite (Tyndale House, 2002)

Osbourn, Derek, 'Introduction to Building' in *Mitchell's Building Series* (Essex: Longman Scientific and Technical, 1985)

Pearsall, Judy (ed.), *Concise Oxford Dictionary* (Oxford: Oxford University Press, 2001)

Pictorial Guide to the Model of Ancient Jerusalem at the Time of the Second Temple (Israel: Holyland Corp.)

Pohle, Peter, and Tim Dowley, *Solomon's Temple Model* (London: Angus Hudson, 2002)

Richman, Chaim, *The Holy Temple of Jerusalem* (Jerusalem: The Temple Institute and Carta, 1997)

Stewart, Andrew, *A House of Prayer* (Darlington: Evangelical Press, 2001)

Tyndale Old Testament and New Testament Commentaries series (Leicester: IVP)

NOTES

1. *Ilumina: digitally animated Bible and encyclopedia suite*, Tyndale House, 2002
2. Alfred Edersheim, *The Temple: Its Ministries and Services*, Hendrickson, Massachusetts, 1994, p. 31
3. Edersheim, *Temple*, pp. 19, 20
4. Edersheim, *Temple*, p. 33
5. *Ilumina*
6. Edersheim, *Temple*, pp. 120, 124–125, 127
7. Edersheim, *Temple*, p. 34
8. Edersheim, *Temple*, p. 127; Chaim Richman, *The Holy Temple of Jerusalem*, The Temple Institute and Carta, Jerusalem, 1997, p. 29
9. Edersheim, *Temple*, p. 142
10. Richman, *Holy Temple*, p. 29
11. Edersheim, *Temple*, pp. 131–132
12. Edersheim, *Temple*, pp. 28–29
13. Edersheim, *Temple*, pp. 61–62, 71–72
14. Edersheim, *Temple*, p. 66
15. Edersheim, *Temple*, p. 25
16. Edersheim, *Temple*, p. 25
17. *Ilumina*
18. Edersheim, *Temple*, p. 20
19. Edersheim, *Temple*, pp. 21–22; *Ilumina*
20. Edersheim, *Temple*, p. 168
21. For example, John Drane (ed.), *The New Lion Encyclopedia of the Bible*, Lion Publishing, Hertfordshire; David and Pat Alexander (eds), *The Lion Handbook to the Bible*, Lion Publishing, Hertfordshire, 1973, 1983
22. Edersheim, *The Temple*, p. 24
23. Edersheim, *The Temple*, pp. 40–43, 111–112.
24. Pat Alexander, *Lion Encyclopedia of the Bible*, Lion Publishing, Hertfordshire p. 25; *Ilumina*
25. *Ilumina*
26. *Collins Dictionary of the English Language*

National Distributors

UK: (and countries not listed below)
CWR, Waverley Abbey House, Waverley Lane, Farnham, Surrey GU9 8EP.
Tel: (01252) 784700 Outside UK (+44) 1252 784700

AUSTRALIA: CMC Australasia, PO Box 519, Belmont, Victoria 3216.
Tel: (03) 5241 3288

CANADA: Cook Communications Ministries, PO Box 98, 55 Woodslee Avenue, Paris, Ontario N3L 3E5.
Tel: 1800 263 2664

GHANA: Challenge Enterprises of Ghana, PO Box 5723, Accra.
Tel: (021) 222437/223249 Fax: (021) 226227

HONG KONG: Cross Communications Ltd, 1/F, 562A Nathan Road, Kowloon.
Tel: 2780 1188 Fax: 2770 6229

INDIA: Crystal Communications, 10-3-18/4/1, East Marredpalli, Secunderabad – 500026, Andhra Pradesh.
Tel/Fax: (040) 27737145

KENYA: Keswick Books and Gifts Ltd, PO Box 10242, Nairobi.
Tel: (02) 331692/226047 Fax: (02) 728557

MALAYSIA: Salvation Book Centre (M) Sdn Bhd, 23 Jalan SS 2/64, 47300 Petaling Jaya, Selangor.
Tel: (03) 78766411/78766797 Fax: (03) 78757066/78756360

NEW ZEALAND: CMC Australasia, PO Box 36015, Lower Hutt.
Tel: 0800 449 408 Fax: 0800 449 049

NIGERIA: FBFM, Helen Baugh House, 96 St Finbarr's College Road, Akoka, Lagos.
Tel: (01) 7747429/4700218/825775/827264

PHILIPPINES: OMF Literature Inc, 776 Boni Avenue, Mandaluyong City.
Tel: (02) 531 2183 Fax: (02) 531 1960

SINGAPORE: Armour Publishing Pte Ltd, Block 203A Henderson Road, 11–06 Henderson Industrial Park, Singapore 159546.
Tel: 6 276 9976 Fax: 6 276 7564

SOUTH AFRICA: Struik Christian Books, 80 MacKenzie Street, PO Box 1144, Cape Town 8000.
Tel: (021) 462 4360 Fax: (021) 461 3612

SRI LANKA: Christombu Books, 27 Hospital Street, Colombo 1.
Tel: (01) 433142/328909

TANZANIA: CLC Christian Book Centre, PO Box 1384, Mkwepu Street, Dar es Salaam.
Tel/Fax: (022) 2119439

USA: Cook Communications Ministries, PO Box 98, 55 Woodslee Avenue, Paris, Ontario N3L 3E5, Canada.
Tel: 1800 263 2664

ZIMBABWE: Word of Life Books (Pvt) Ltd, Christian Media Centre, 8 Aberdeen Road, Avondale, PO Box A480 Avondale, Harare, Zimbabwe.
Tel: (04) 333355 or 091301188

For email addresses, visit the CWR website: www.cwr.org.uk

CWR is a registered charity – Number 294387

CWR is a limited company registered in England – Registration Number 1990308

Cover to Cover Bible Study

The Tabernacle
Ian Sewter

This Bible study guide will help you:

- develop an understanding of the Bible in a new and fresh way by seeing the intriguing significance of the Tabernacle in Scripture
- expand your view of the New Testament in light of the revelations from the Old

ISBN: 1-85345-230-0

The Covenants
John Houghton

This exciting study will:

- reveal how God's character unfolds through the Bible in the various promises He has made
- be inspired as you discover the God of covenant love, life, providence faith, law, Kingship and grace

ISBN: 1-85345-255-6

Part of the 30-book Cover to Cover Bible Study series

£3.99 each (plus p&p)

Price correct at time of going to print

Pocket devotionals from Selwyn Hughes

- Two beautifully presented devotional publications containing thoughts for the whole year from the pen of Selwyn Hughes.
- Designed to help you grow in your relationship with Jesus and enhance your spiritual journey.
- These pocket-sized books make ideal travelling companions or attractive gifts for friends or relatives.

Growing in Christ
ISBN: 1-85345-345-5

Caring for the Soul
ISBN: 1-85345-346-3

£6.99 each (plus p&p)

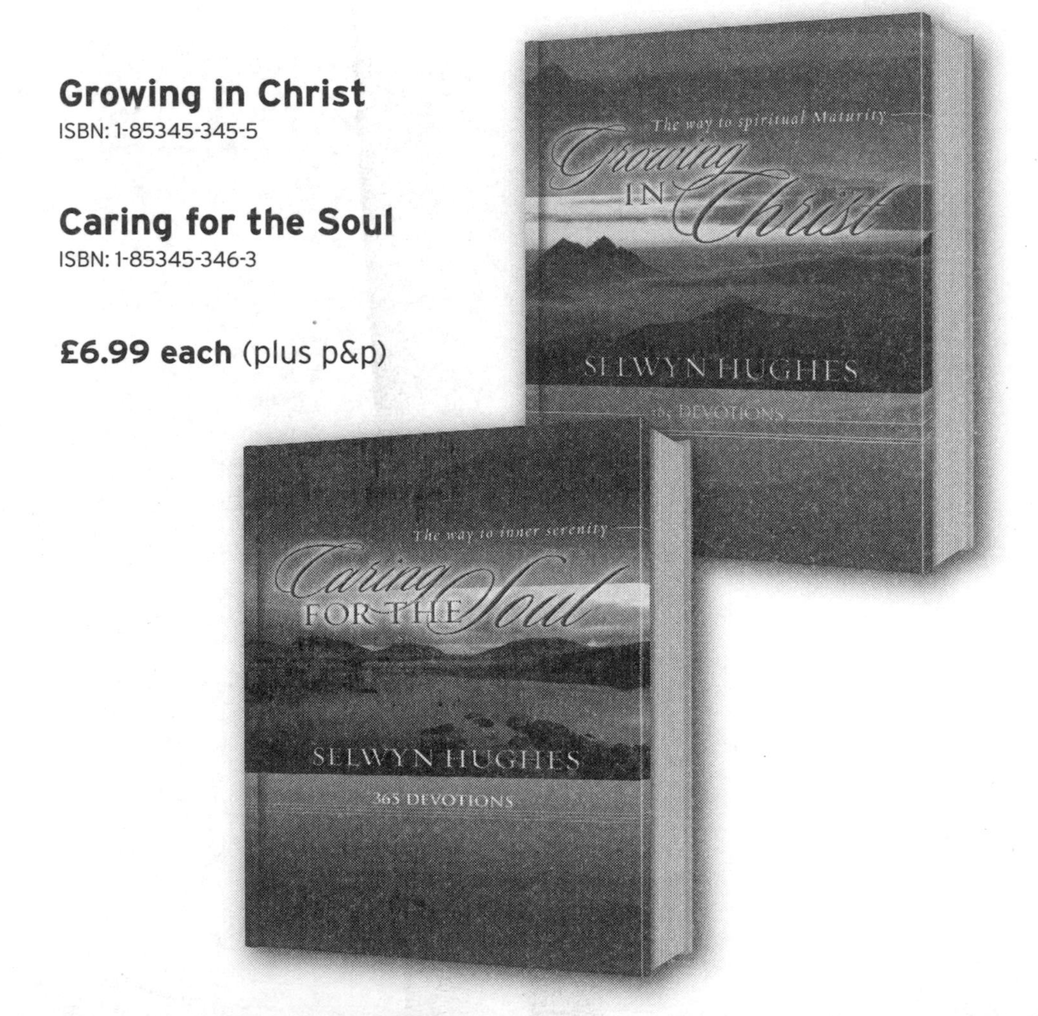

Price correct at time of going to print